Contents

CW01025225

Both Australia and New Zealand claim the pavlova, named after a Russian ballet dancer, as their own.

AUSTRA

Darwin

AUSTRALIA

Perth

Brisbane

Adelaide

Melbourne

Sydney

Hobart

Walkway to... BEACH

LIA

ZUCCHINI SLICE

*

PUMPKIN SOUP WITH
SAGE DAMPER

*

BARBECUED PRAWN
SKEWERS WITH MANGO
AND AVOCADO SALSA

*

MINI BACON AND
ROSEMARY MEATLOAVES

*

ANZAC BISCUITS

*

TROPICAL FRUIT PAVLOVA
WITH LIME AND MINT

AUSTRALIA COOKING NOTES

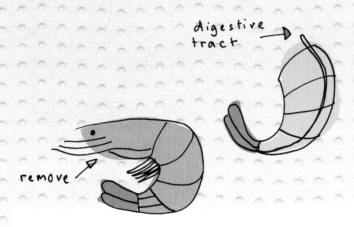

digestive tract

remove

PUMPKIN SOUP WITH A TWIST

To make a spicy pumpkin soup, follow the recipe on page 10 and add 2 tsp red curry paste to onion and garlic. Omit bay leaves and mixed spice. Reduce quantity of stock to 375ml (1½ cups) and add a 400ml can coconut milk. Serve drizzled with coconut cream and sprinkled with toasted shredded coconut.

butternut

queensland blue

Peeling and cleaning prawns

First twist the head. Peel the shell and the legs and, if removing the tail, squeeze it and pull it gently from the body. To remove the digestive tract, using a sharp knife, score down the back to expose the dark 'vein' and pull it out. To remove the digestive tract without cutting along the back of the prawn, carefully pull out the vein through the opening at the head.

Removing mango flesh

Place mango on a chopping board. Using a sharp knife, cut lengthwise down one side of the stone – if you feel some resistance, you are too close to the stone, so shift the knife slightly. Repeat on the other side to get 2 cheeks. To peel, hold mango cheek in your hand, skin-side down. Slide a large spoon (or a glass or beaker, as in the picture, left) just inside the skin and scoop the flesh out in one piece.

Separating eggs for egg whites

Have 2 small bowls ready. Crack 1 egg on the side of a bowl. Pull the two sides apart, carefully pouring the egg white into the bowl, while keeping the yolk in the shell, using the other shell as a strainer. Always break eggs into a separate bowl before adding to the main mixture; that way, you can make sure that the eggs are fresh and no bits of shell get in.

ANZAC BISCUITS These Aussie favourites were first made to send to the Australian and New Zealand Army Corps (ANZAC) during World War I. They have excellent keeping qualities – perfect for long journeys!

SOAKING BAMBOO SKEWERS

Before you thread food onto bamboo skewers, soak them in water for 30 minutes. This will stop them igniting on the barbecue or chargrill. Bamboo skewers are available in packs from supermarkets. You can also use metal skewers, available from kitchen suppliers. These also help to cook the food by conducting heat through the centre, so you need to make sure you're wearing oven gloves when turning them, as the metal will get very hot.

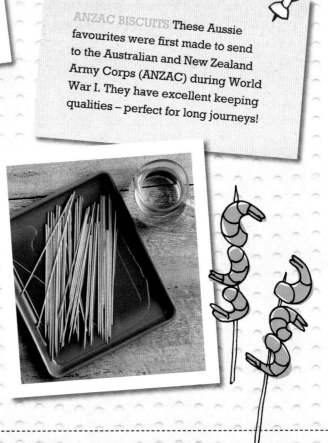

zucchini slice

Serves: 4
Preparation: 15 mins
Cooking: 40 mins

1 tbs olive oil
1 onion, chopped
1 short-cut rindless bacon
  rasher, chopped
5 eggs, lightly beaten
75g (½ cup) self-raising
  flour
5 (400g) small zucchinis,
  coarsely grated
160g (1⅓ cups) grated
  cheddar
12 grape tomatoes, halved

1 Preheat oven to 180C. Lightly grease a 20cm square cake or slice pan. Line base and sides with baking paper. Heat oil in a frying pan over low–medium heat. Add onion and cook, stirring, for 5 minutes or until softened. Add bacon and cook, stirring, for 5 minutes or until browned. Set aside for 5 minutes to cool.

2 Combine eggs and flour in a bowl and whisk gently until almost smooth. Add zucchinis, onion mixture and 120g (1 cup) grated cheese. Stir gently to combine. Season with salt and pepper. Pour mixture into prepared pan, smooth surface and scatter with remaining cheese. Press tomatoes, cut-side up, evenly spaced apart, onto surface. Bake for 30 minutes or until set and golden. Cool slightly before cutting into squares to serve.

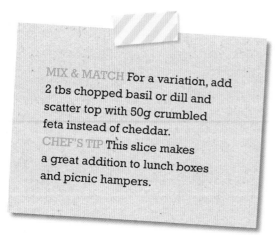

MIX & MATCH For a variation, add 2 tbs chopped basil or dill and scatter top with 50g crumbled feta instead of cheddar.
CHEF'S TIP This slice makes a great addition to lunch boxes and picnic hampers.

pumpkin soup with sage damper

Serves: 4
Preparation: 30 mins
Cooking: 50 mins

1 tbs olive oil
1 onion, chopped
2 cloves garlic, crushed
1.3kg pumpkin, peeled,
    seeded, chopped (get
    an adult to help you)
750ml (3 cups) chicken
    or vegetable stock
2 fresh bay leaves
60ml (¼ cup) thickened
    cream
½ tsp mixed spice

Sage damper
450g (3 cups)
    self-raising flour
80g cold butter, chopped
1 tbs chopped sage, plus
    8 sage leaves, extra
310ml (1¼ cups) buttermilk

1 Heat oil in a saucepan over medium heat. Add onion and cook, stirring occasionally, for 5 minutes or until soft. Add garlic and cook, stirring occasionally, for 1 minute or until fragrant. Add pumpkin, stock and bay leaves. Bring to the boil, then reduce heat and simmer for 15 minutes or until tender. Set aside for 10 minutes to cool slightly. Discard bay leaves. Reserve 180ml (¾ cup) liquid.

2 Using a stick blender, blend soup until smooth. (Alternatively, process soup, in batches, in a food processor until smooth.) Stir in cream and mixed spice. Add reserved liquid to thin the soup, if necessary. Season with salt and pepper.

3 To make sage damper, preheat oven to 200C and line an oven tray with baking paper. Sift flour and a pinch of salt into a bowl. Using fingertips, rub in the butter until mixture resembles breadcrumbs. Stir in chopped sage. Using a butter knife, gradually stir in buttermilk until the mixture just comes together. Turn out dough onto a lightly floured surface and knead gently with your fingertips for 2 minutes or until almost smooth (don't over-knead the dough or the damper will be tough). Pat into a 17cm round. Place damper on prepared oven tray. Using a small, sharp knife, make 8 cuts, 2mm deep, in the top of dough to create 8 wedges. Place 1 extra sage leaf on each wedge, pressing lightly to stick. Bake damper for 30 minutes or until golden and loaf sounds hollow when tapped.

4 Stir soup over low heat until heated through, then serve with warm sage damper.

MIX & MATCH For an Indian version, add 2 tsp grated ginger and 2 tsp mild curry powder to the onion and garlic. Serve with a spoonful of yoghurt and scatter with chopped coriander leaves.

barbecued prawn skewers with mango and avocado salsa

Serves: 4
Preparation: 20 mins
Cooking: 8 mins

24 (about 1kg) large green
   king prawns, peeled,
   cleaned, leaving
   tails intact*
1 tbs olive oil
2 cloves garlic, crushed
1 tbs lime juice
8 bamboo skewers*, soaked
   in water for 30 minutes,
   drained

Mango and avocado salsa

1 large mango*, peeled, cut
   into 1cm pieces
1 large avocado, stone
   removed, peeled, cut into
   1cm pieces (see Mexican
   Cooking Notes, p 190)
½ small red onion,
   finely chopped
1 tsp finely grated lime zest
1 tbs lime juice
1 tsp finely grated ginger
1 tbs chopped mint
1 tbs chopped coriander
1 tbs sweet chilli sauce

1 To make mango and avocado salsa, combine all ingredients in a bowl. Season with salt and pepper. Set aside until needed.

2 Preheat barbecue or chargrill to high. Combine prawns, oil, garlic and lime juice in a bowl and season with salt and pepper. Thread a skewer close to the edge of the prawn tail through to the top of prawn, then repeat with 2 more prawns. Repeat with remaining skewers and prawns.

3 Cook prawn skewers, in 2 batches, for 2 minutes each side or until prawns change in colour and are cooked through. Serve prawn skewers with mango and avocado salsa.

*See Cooking Notes, p 6

MIX & MATCH If you prefer, substitute 600g chicken thigh fillets, cut into 3cm pieces, for the prawns.

mini bacon and rosemary meatloaves

Makes: 4

Preparation: 20 mins

Cooking: 30 mins

1 red onion, grated
1 small carrot, grated
600g minced beef
1 egg
55g (¾ cup) fresh
    breadcrumbs (see Italian
    Cooking Notes, p 38)
2 tbs barbecue sauce
2 cloves garlic, crushed
1 tbs chopped rosemary
    leaves, plus 4 small
    rosemary sprigs, extra
4 slices rindless middle
    bacon rashers, halved
    lengthwise

Roasted sweet potatoes
and red onion

500g sweet potatoes,
    peeled, cut into 3cm
    pieces
2 red onions, each cut into
    6 wedges
1 tbs olive oil

1 Preheat oven to 180C. Lightly spray 4 holes of a 180ml (¾-cup) Texas muffin pan with oil. Place onion, carrot, mince, egg, breadcrumbs, barbecue sauce, garlic and chopped rosemary leaves in a large bowl. Season with salt and pepper. Using your hands, mix until well combined.

2 Place 1 halved slice of bacon in a muffin hole, leaving the ends overhanging edge. Place a second halved slice widthwise on top, leaving ends overhanging the edge. Fill hole with one-quarter of the mince mixture, pressing down firmly, then fold bacon slices over. Place a small sprig of rosemary on top of bacon. Repeat with remaining bacon, mince mixture and rosemary sprigs.

3 To make roasted sweet potatoes and red onion, toss sweet potatoes and onions on a lightly oiled oven tray. Season with salt and pepper. Roast meatloaves and vegetables for 30 minutes or until vegetables are browned and juices run clear when a skewer is inserted into centre of each meatloaf.

CHEF'S TIP To make a whole meatloaf, line a 1.25L (5-cup) loaf pan with whole rindless bacon rashers and fill with mince mixture as in step 2. Continue as per recipe, roasting for 50 minutes.

anzac biscuits

Makes: 30
Preparation: 15 mins
+ 5 mins cooling time
Cooking: 15 mins

220g (1 cup, firmly packed)
   brown sugar
90g (1 cup) rolled oats
150g (1 cup) plain
   flour, sifted
80g (1 cup) desiccated
   coconut
175g butter, chopped
2 tbs golden syrup
½ tsp bicarbonate of soda

1 Preheat oven to 170C. Line 2 oven trays with baking paper. Combine sugar, oats, flour and coconut in a bowl. Heat butter and golden syrup with 1 tbs water in a saucepan over low heat, stirring until melted. Carefully add bicarbonate of soda (mixture will froth). Pour butter mixture into flour mixture and stir to combine.

2 Form level tablespoons of mixture into balls and place on prepared trays 5cm apart. Flatten balls slightly with a fork. Bake for 15 minutes or until deep golden, swapping trays halfway. Cool biscuits for 5 minutes on trays before transferring to a wire rack and cooling completely.

CHEF'S TIP The cooking time will determine the crispness of the biscuits. They will still feel soft to the touch when cooked and will firm up on cooling. For a chewier style of biscuit, cook until light golden in colour. For a crunchier version, cook until biscuits are deep golden in colour. The biscuits will lose their crispness over time if not stored in an airtight container.

MIX & MATCH For a spicier variation, add ½ tsp ground ginger to the flour mixture.

tropical fruit pavlova with lime and mint

Serves: 6
Preparation: 30 mins
+ 3 hrs cooling time
Cooking: 1 hr 15 mins

4 egg whites*, at room
   temperature
220g (1 cup) caster sugar
3 tsp cornflour
1 tsp white vinegar
1 small mango*, peeled,
   sliced into thin strips
½ small pineapple,
   peeled, cored, cut
   into thin strips (get an
   adult to help you)
Pulp of 2 passionfruit
Extra mint leaves, to serve

Lime cream
300ml thickened cream
1 tsp finely grated lime zest
2 tsp lime juice
1½ tbs icing sugar
1 tbs chopped mint

1 Preheat oven to 110C. Line an oven tray with baking paper. Place an 18cm plate or bowl in the centre of the paper, then, using a pencil, trace around the plate to mark an 18cm circle. Turn baking paper over so that pencil side is underneath. Using an electric mixer, beat egg whites until soft peaks form. With motor running, gradually add sugar, 1 tablespoon at a time. Beat for 10 minutes or until sugar has dissolved and mixture is thick and glossy. Using a metal spatula, fold in cornflour and vinegar.

2 Spoon mixture to cover the circle on the baking paper, using a metal spatula to form a mound with high sides and a flattish top. Bake for 1 hour 15 minutes or until pavlova is dry and firm to the touch. Turn off oven. Use a wooden spoon to hold the oven door ajar and leave the pavlova in the oven to cool for 3 hours (this helps the pavlova dry slowly and evenly to a crisp texture).

3 Meanwhile, to make lime cream, using an electric mixer, whisk cream and lime zest to form soft peaks. Fold in lime juice, sugar and chopped mint. Cover and refrigerate until needed.

4 To serve, spread top of pavlova with lime cream. Decorate with mango and pineapple, and drizzle with passionfruit pulp. Scatter with extra mint leaves.

*See Cooking Notes, p 6

CHEF'S TIP The secret to a good meringue is to whisk a lot of air into the egg whites. Any trace of fat from a dirty bowl or a bit of yolk will prevent this. When beating, if the mixture forms a peak and folds over, this is a soft peak. If it forms a peak that stays upright, this is a firm peak.

SPAIN

Flamenco
dancing
Olé!

The Spanish say
'Buen apetito!'
before a meal!

San Sebastián

Barcelona

Madrid

Valencia

Ibiza

SPAIN

TOSTADAS
*
MARINATED
GREEN OLIVES
*
GARLIC PRAWNS
*
MEATBALLS IN SPICY
TOMATO SAUCE
*
SPANISH TORTILLA
*
CHICKEN PAELLA
*
ORANGE
CARAMEL FLAN

SPAIN COOKING NOTES

Spanish produce

Jamón The most prized variety of this cured ham is made from pigs that feed on acorns (*jamón ibérico de bellota*). Available from selected delis. Substitute with prosciutto.
Manchego A hard sheep's milk cheese, from the La Mancha region in Spain.
Chorizo A pork sausage, available fresh or cured. Smoked paprika gives them their distinctive colour and flavour.

TAPAS These small sharing plates come in many forms, such as the meatballs, or *albóndigas*, on page 28. The word 'tapas' comes from the Spanish word *tapar* (to cover). One theory is that tapas originated in Spanish taverns, where slices of bread or meat (usually ham or chorizo) were used to cover the tops of sherry glasses to ward off flies.

SAFFRON

The world's most expensive spice is made from the hand-harvested stigmas of crocus flowers. It has been highly prized for centuries and is also used as a dye and in medicines. It is grown in countries including Iran, Greece, India and Spain, and, more recently, in Tasmania.

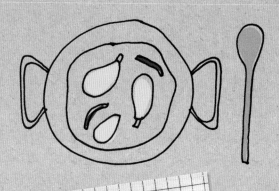

Viva socarrat!

For many paella lovers, the best part of the dish is the crunchy, chewy crust that forms on the base of the pan as the rice cooks. It's called socarrat, and is highly prized. That's why it's important not to stir the paella as you're cooking it, to allow this flavour-filled layer of rice to settle and cook to a golden crust. The pan you use makes all the difference (see left) and so does the *sofrito* or tomato, onion and garlic sauce that you cook first before adding the other ingredients. Traditionally, there should be about 1.5cm of rice in the pan once your paella is cooked. The best rice to use is a Spanish variety, Calasparra, available from delis and specialist food shops, but we used arborio rice in our paella recipe, page 32.

PAELLA PAN Traditional paella pans come in various sizes and are designed to be used over a gas flame. They are available from kitchenware stores. A heavy-based frying pan will work just as well with a gas or electric hotplate. And remember, paella should be brought to the table and served straight from the pan.

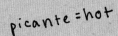

picante = hot

dulce = sweet

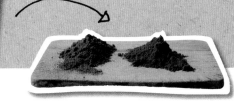

Paprika

Smoked Spanish paprika (*pimentón*) is made from ground dried red peppers. It comes in several varieties, including sweet (*dulce*), bittersweet (*agridulce*) and hot (*picante*). We've used the sweet variety in our recipes, which is available from supermarkets and specialist food shops.

tostadas

Makes: 8
Preparation: 10 mins
Cooking: 10 mins

½ baguette
2 tbs extra virgin olive oil
1 large ripe tomato, halved
4 thin slices jamón*
   or prosciutto
4 thin slices manchego*

Preheat grill to high or heat a lightly oiled chargrill. Using a serrated bread knife, cut baguette on the diagonal into 8 x 1.5cm–thick slices. Grill or chargrill the bread for 1 minute each side or until toasted. Brush one side with olive oil and rub with cut side of the tomato, squeezing tomato to extract as much juice as possible. Place jamón on 4 of the tostadas and manchego on the remainder. Serve tostadas warm.

See Cooking Notes, p 22

marinated green olives

Serves: 4
Preparation: 10 mins

2 tsp fennel seeds
3 small cloves garlic
¼ cup rosemary leaves
3 tsp thyme leaves
4 small fresh bay leaves, or
   2 large leaves, torn in half
400g pitted green olives
   or pimiento-stuffed green
   olives (see Chef's Tip)
160ml (⅔ cup) olive oil
80ml (⅓ cup) sunflower oil

Using a mortar and pestle (see Thai Cooking Notes, p 172), grind fennel seeds to release oils, then transfer to a bowl. Lightly crush garlic with the mortar and pestle until they split. Add to fennel seeds. Add rosemary, thyme, bay leaves and olives to the bowl and combine. Spoon into a clean, dry 650ml screw-top jar and pour in oils. Seal and refrigerate for up to 3 weeks.

CHEF'S TIP Keeping the olives well covered with olive oil in the refrigerator will preserve them. The oil may solidify slightly, forming little beads of solid oil. Remove from fridge and stand at room temperature for 1 hour to allow oil to warm up and return to liquid.

garlic prawns

Serves: 4
Preparation: 30 mins
Cooking: 5 mins

1kg medium green prawns,
    peeled, cleaned, leaving
    tails intact (see Australian
    Cooking Notes, p 6)
50g butter
80ml (⅓ cup) olive oil
4 cloves garlic, crushed
½ tsp sweet paprika (see
    Cooking Notes, p 22)
¼ tsp chilli flakes
2 tbs lemon juice
2 tbs chopped
    flat-leaf parsley
Lemon wedges and
    crusty bread, to serve

1 Place prawns in a large bowl, add ½ tsp salt and toss to combine.

2 Heat the butter, oil, garlic, paprika, chilli, ¼ tsp salt and lemon juice in a frying pan over medium heat. When foaming, add the prawns and cook, turning occasionally, for 5 minutes or until they curl up and change colour.

3 Sprinkle with parsley and serve, while still sizzling, with lemon wedges and plenty of crusty bread to mop up the juices.

TIME SAVER Buy 500g peeled, cleaned prawns from the fishmonger instead of 1kg whole prawns.

CHEF'S TIP

For a spicier dish, increase the chilli to ¾ tsp, and for a milder heat, reduce the chilli to a pinch. To measure a pinch, use the tip of a knife or spoon to remove chilli flakes from the jar.

meatballs in spicy tomato sauce

Makes: 20

Preparation: 40 mins

+ 30 mins chilling time

Cooking: 35 mins

200g minced pork

200g minced veal

3 cloves garlic, crushed

½ tsp sweet paprika

1 tsp ground coriander

1 tsp ground cumin

1 pinch ground cinnamon

70g (1 cup) fresh
breadcrumbs (see Italian
Cooking Notes, p 38)

2 eggs, lightly beaten

2 tbs olive oil

40g (⅓ cup) frozen peas

Crusty bread, to serve

Spicy tomato sauce

1 tbs olive oil

1 onion, finely chopped

1 pinch ground chilli

500ml (2 cups) tomato
passata (sieved
puréed tomatoes)

125ml (½ cup) chicken stock

½ tsp sugar

1 Combine both minces, garlic, spices, breadcrumbs and eggs in a bowl and season well with salt and pepper. Using your hands, mix until well combined. Using a measuring spoon and spatula, scoop out level tablespoons of mixture, roll into balls and place on a plate. Cover with plastic wrap and refrigerate for 30 minutes or until firm. Heat 1 tbs olive oil in a non-stick frying pan and cook half the meatballs over medium–high heat for 2 minutes, turning frequently, or until browned. Drain on paper towel. Add a little more oil to the pan if necessary and repeat with remaining meatballs.

2 To make sauce, heat oil in a large saucepan over medium heat, add the onion and cook, stirring occasionally, for 5 minutes or until softened. Add the chilli and cook, stirring, for 1 minute. Increase heat to high, add tomato passata and stock, and bring to the boil. Reduce heat to medium, then simmer, uncovered, for 10 minutes. Stir in sugar and season with salt and pepper.

3 Add meatballs to sauce, simmer, uncovered, for 5 minutes, gently shaking pan to turn meatballs and coat with sauce. Cook for a further 5 minutes or until sauce is thick and meatballs are cooked through. Add peas and simmer for a further 3 minutes or until heated through. Serve hot with crusty bread.

TIME SAVER This dish can be made up to 3 days ahead and kept covered in the refrigerator.

spanish tortilla

Serves: 6–8
Preparation: 15 mins
+ 20 mins cooling time
Cooking: 1 hr

650g desiree potatoes
2 large onions
60ml (¼ cup) olive oil
4 eggs

1 Preheat oven to 200C. Lightly oil a 20cm round cake pan. Line base with baking paper. Peel potatoes and, using a food processor fitted with the slicing attachment, slice potatoes and onions. Place potatoes and onions in a large bowl, add oil and toss to coat. Spread potato mixture over a large oven tray, cover with foil and roast for 30 minutes or until potatoes are just tender when pierced with a skewer. Cool for 10 minutes.

2 Place eggs in a large bowl, season with ½ tsp salt and ½ tsp pepper and whisk to combine. Add the cooled potato mixture and gently stir until well combined. It doesn't matter if the potato breaks up a little. Spoon the potato and egg mixture into prepared pan, pressing down to even out potatoes in the pan. Bake for 30 minutes or until set. Stand pan on a wire rack for 10 minutes. Run a small knife around the edge of the pan and turn out tortilla onto a large plate. Cut into wedges to serve.

CHEF'S TIP To make the tortilla the traditional way in a frying pan, heat 1 tbs olive oil in a large, non-stick frying pan over medium–high heat. Spoon egg and potato mixture into pan and press down with the back of the spoon to even out the mixture. Cover with a lid or foil and cook over low heat for 10 minutes or until set and tortilla moves about freely when frying pan is gently shaken. Stand for 5 minutes before inverting onto a large plate.

CHEF'S TIP If your food processor has a thick and a thin slicing attachment, use the thicker attachment to prevent potatoes breaking up too much. The potatoes can also be cut with a knife into 3mm-thick pieces.

chicken paella

Serves: 4–6
Preparation: 25 mins
Cooking: 1 hr 10 mins

½ tsp saffron threads*
2 tsp sweet Hungarian
   paprika
2 tsp smoked Spanish
   paprika*
¼ tsp dried chilli flakes
2 tbs chopped flat-leaf
   parsley
2 ripe tomatoes,
   roughly chopped
1 tbs red wine vinegar
2 cloves garlic
1 small red onion, quartered
½ lemon, juiced
2 tbs olive oil
3 chicken 'lovely legs'
3 chicken drumettes
1 small red capsicum,
   cut into strips
150g green beans,
   trimmed, halved
150g arborio rice
1 (175g) chorizo sausage*,
   thinly sliced
250ml (1 cup) chicken stock

1 Using a mortar and pestle (see Thai Cooking Notes, p 172), grind saffron threads until the strands are coarsely crushed. Add 1 tbs hot water and leave for 10 minutes to infuse. Place the saffron and liquid, paprikas, chilli, half of the parsley, tomatoes, vinegar, garlic and onion in a blender or food processor. Add lemon juice, 1 tsp salt and ½ tsp black pepper, and process until smooth.

2 Heat oil in a 30cm (base measurement) paella pan or large, deep heavy-based frying pan over medium–high heat. Add chicken and cook for 5 minutes each side or until browned. Transfer to a plate. Reduce heat to medium, add capsicum and beans, and cook, stirring, for 5 minutes or until starting to soften. Add rice and chorizo and cook, stirring, for 1 minute or until rice is opaque. Increase heat to high, add tomato mixture and cook, stirring, for 1 minute or until bubbling and fragrant.

3 Stir in 200ml chicken stock and bring to the boil. Reduce heat to low–medium until gently simmering. Place chicken pieces on rice in pan and cook, uncovered, for 55 minutes without stirring. Check to see if there is any liquid. If not, pour remaining stock around edge of pan. Cook for a further 5 minutes or until rice is just tender – it should still have a slight bite to it. Remove from heat, scatter with remaining 1 tbs parsley and stand for 5 minutes before serving straight from the pan.

*See Cooking Notes, p 22

orange caramel flan

Serves: 8
....
Preparation: 15 mins
+ 1 hr 30 mins cooling time
+ 6 hrs refrigeration time
....
Cooking: 1 hr 20 mins
....

300g (1⅓ cups) caster sugar
450ml milk
300ml pouring cream
3 tsp finely grated
   orange zest
7 eggs, at room
   temperature

CHEF'S TIPS
• Don't grease the cake
pan or use a non-stick
cake pan, as the caramel
will not cling to it.
• To test if the caramel
flan is set, insert
a small knife in the
centre. If the custard
stays separate when
you move the knife to
the side and the knife
comes out clean or with
a little softly set custard,
the custard is set.

1 Preheat oven to 200C. Place 1 oven shelf in the middle to lower half of the oven and remove all other shelves above it. Line the base of a large roasting pan with a clean folded tea towel. Combine 150g (⅔ cup) sugar and 60ml (¼ cup) water in a small saucepan and cook over low heat, stirring, until the sugar dissolves. Increase heat to high and bring to the boil, brushing down side of the pan with a wet pastry brush to remove any sugar crystals. Boil, uncovered, without stirring, for 5 minutes or until the caramel is dark golden. (When the caramel begins to colour, watch it carefully as it will change colour in a matter of seconds.) Remove from heat and pour into a deep 20cm round cake pan (see Chef's Tips). Ask an adult to hold the cake pan with a tea towel, as it will be hot, then to swirl it until the base is well coated with caramel. Place in the roasting pan.

2 Combine the milk, cream and zest in a saucepan. Cook gently over medium heat for 5 minutes. Do not boil. Remove from heat and stand for 5 minutes to cool slightly. Strain.

3 Place eggs and remaining 150g (⅔ cup) sugar in a large, heatproof bowl and stir with a wooden spoon until well combined. Place bowl of egg mixture on a damp cloth to keep it steady. Stirring continuously, gradually pour in the warm cream mixture. Pour the mixture over the caramel in the cake pan. Fill the roasting pan with enough hot water to come halfway up the side of the cake pan. Cover cake pan loosely with foil.

4 Carefully place roasting pan in oven, then reduce temperature to 160C. Bake for 1 hour and 10 minutes or until set (see Chef's Tips). Turn off oven, use a wooden spoon to prop door open slightly and cool caramel flan in oven for 30 minutes. Remove cake pan from roasting pan and stand for 1 hour to cool. Cover with plastic wrap and refrigerate for 6 hours or overnight. To serve, gently run a thin, sharp knife around the side to loosen flan, then carefully invert onto a large, lipped plate.

Lunch is usually the main meal of the day in Italy.

ITALY

ITALY

Milan · Venice

Florence

Rome · Naples

Sicily

POTATO GNOCCHI
WITH PANCETTA
✳
CHICKEN CACCIATORE
✳
PUMPKIN RISOTTO
✳
SPAGHETTI
WITH PESTO
✳
EGGPLANT PARMIGIANA
✳
LEMON SORBETTO
✳
CASSATA CAKE

'La cucina
di casa' means
'home cooking'
in Italian.

ITALY COOKING NOTES

MAKING BREADCRUMBS

To make fresh breadcrumbs, use white or wholemeal bread that's at least a day old (fresh bread tends to be a little too moist to make good, consistent breadcrumbs). Remove crusts and discard, then tear bread into large pieces. Process bread in a food processor until fine crumbs form. Store breadcrumbs in an airtight container in the freezer for up to one month.

Roasting pine nuts

Place the pine nuts in a frying pan without any oil over medium heat and cook, stirring or tossing continuously, for 2 minutes or until golden. Be sure to keep the pine nuts moving and turning in the pan. That's because they have a high oil content, which means they can 'catch' or burn very quickly.

Italian cheeses

Parmesan A hard, cooked cow's milk cheese that's aged for at least 12 months. It originates from Northern Italy and, while it's made elsewhere, only the authentic Italian version can go by its official name, Parmigano Reggiano.

Bocconcini Small, mild white cheese 'balls' made from buffalo's or cow's milk. They're sold packed in water or whey.

Fresh ricotta Available from the deli section of supermarkets, it's drier, firmer and tastes creamier than packaged ricotta.

Assembling the cassata

This special Easter cake is originally from Sicily. The sponge is usually soaked in a liqueur, then sandwiched together with a delicious filling of fresh sweetened ricotta, chopped chocolate and candied (or glacé) fruit. The whole cake is then covered with fondant icing or marzipan, which is usually tinted a lovely pale green. Finally, the cake is topped with piles of candied (or glacé) fruit. The sponge is used to line the base and sides of the pan and is then liberally brushed with orange juice before being filled.

AL DENTE This Italian term means 'to the tooth' or 'to the bite', and describes the texture of pasta when it's cooked just right. To check, bite down on a piece of pasta – it should be soft, but still have a little firmness.

ARBORIO RICE

Arborio rice is a short-grain rice which gives risotto its beautiful creamy texture. Carnaroli and vialone nano rice, both available from delis, are the stars of risotto-making, but are more expensive. The creaminess of risotto comes from the starches released when the rice is stirred or shaken as hot stock is absorbed. Ideally, this is balanced by the individual grains still being slightly al dente (see note above).

arborio rice

potato gnocchi
with pancetta

Serves: 4

Preparation: 30 mins

Cooking: 40 mins

600g potatoes,
   such as desiree,
   Dutch cream, pink eye
40g butter, melted
225g (1½ cups) plain flour
1 tbs olive oil
6 thin slices pancetta
150g butter, chopped
1 large leek, trimmed,
   halved lengthwise,
   thinly sliced
¼ cup small sage leaves
1 tbs pine nuts, roasted
   (see Cooking Notes, p 38)

1 Place unpeeled potatoes in a large saucepan, cover with plenty of cold water and add a pinch of salt. Bring to the boil and cook for 25 minutes or until tender. Drain and cool for 5 minutes. When cool enough to handle, peel away skin.

2 Place hot peeled potatoes in a bowl and, using a potato masher, mash until smooth. Add melted butter, season with salt and pepper, and mash to combine.

3 Lightly dust a clean work surface with 2 tbs flour. Tip potato onto floured work surface. Add two-thirds of remaining flour and, using your hands, mix it in to form a soft dough, adding more flour if necessary. Knead the mixture for 4 minutes or until smooth. Divide dough into 3, roll each piece into a sausage shape about 2cm in diameter, then cut into 3cm-long pieces.

4 Preheat oven to 150C and warm a lightly oiled ovenproof dish. Bring a large saucepan of water to the boil, add a pinch of salt. Add one-third of the gnocchi to water, return water to a fast simmer and cook for 3 minutes or until gnocchi rise to the surface. Using a slotted spoon, transfer gnocchi to warmed dish. Repeat with remaining gnocchi.

5 Meanwhile, to make sauce, heat oil in a frying pan and cook pancetta over medium heat for 3 minutes or until crisp. Drain on paper towel. Break into pieces. Turn heat down to low, add 50g chopped butter to pan and, when melted, add leek and cook, stirring occasionally, for 3 minutes or until softened. Heat remaining 100g butter in a small frying pan over medium heat for 1 minute or until foaming and golden, then add the sage leaves and pine nuts, and cook for 30 seconds. Add torn pancetta with leek to gnocchi, then toss gently. Serve immediately, scattered with sage leaves and pine nuts.

CHEF'S TIP Cook gnocchi in fast simmering water, not boiling water. If the water is boiling rapidly, the gnocchi will fall apart. MIX & MATCH Serve gnocchi with pesto and sautéed prawns.

chicken cacciatore

Serves: 4
Preparation: 10 mins
Cooking: 55 mins

4 chicken drumsticks
4 chicken thigh fillets
2 tbs olive oil
1 large onion, chopped
4 cloves garlic, finely
    chopped
150ml red wine
2 x 400g cans
    chopped tomatoes
180ml (¾ cup)
    chicken stock
4 fresh bay leaves
2 sprigs rosemary
120g (1 cup) pitted
    black olives
¼ cup chopped flat-leaf
    parsley
2 x 400g cans cannellini
    beans, drained, rinsed
Instant polenta, prepared
    according to packet
    instructions, to serve

1 Preheat oven to 180C. Season chicken pieces with salt and
pepper. Heat 1 tbs oil in an ovenproof frying pan over medium
heat, then cook chicken, in batches, for 2 minutes each side or
until browned. Transfer chicken to a plate.

2 Add remaining 1 tbs oil to pan, then add onion and garlic,
and cook for 10 minutes or until softened. Add wine and
cook, stirring, scraping any brown pieces from base of the
pan. Stir in tomatoes, stock, bay leaves and rosemary sprigs,
bring to a simmer and cook for 3 minutes. Return chicken to pan
and bring to the boil.

3 Cover with a lid or foil and cook in oven for 30 minutes.
Pierce the thickest part of chicken thigh with a skewer and
if juices are clear, chicken is cooked. If juices are pink, return
chicken to the oven and cook for a further 10 minutes. Stir in
olives, three-quarters of the parsley and the beans and cook
for a further 3 minutes or until beans are heated through.
Check seasoning and stand, covered, for 5 minutes. Scatter
casserole with remaining parsley. Serve with polenta.

pumpkin risotto

Serves: 4
Preparation: 15 mins
Cooking: 30 mins

1.25 litres (5 cups)
   chicken stock
50g butter
1 tbs olive oil
1 large onion, finely chopped
2 cloves garlic, crushed
150g peeled, seeded
   chopped butternut
   pumpkin
300g (1½ cups) arborio
   rice*
150g (1 cup) cooked puréed
   butternut pumpkin
   (see Chef's Tip)
1 tbs chopped flat-leaf
   parsley
1 tbs chopped sage
20g (¼ cup) grated
   parmesan*
Shaved parmesan, to serve

1 Place stock in a saucepan and bring to a simmer over low heat, then reduce heat to very low to keep stock warm. Heat 30g of the butter and oil over medium heat in a separate saucepan. Add onion and cook, stirring occasionally, for 5 minutes or until softened. Add garlic and chopped pumpkin and cook, stirring occasionally, for 4 minutes. Increase heat to medium, add the rice and stir to coat in mixture, then cook, stirring, for 1 minute.

2 Reduce heat to low–medium. Add 125ml (½ cup) hot stock to rice mixture and cook, stirring continuously, for 3 minutes or until stock is absorbed. Continue adding more stock, 250ml (1 cup) at a time, stirring until stock is absorbed, before adding next amount of stock. This will take about 20 minutes. Check rice by squeezing a grain between your fingers – if it breaks and feels soft but still has a little give, it is ready. There may be some stock left at this stage. If rice is still firm, continue to add stock and stir. The risotto should be creamy and glossy.

3 Add puréed pumpkin, chopped herbs, grated parmesan and remaining 20g butter and stir well to combine. Season with salt and pepper. Remove from heat and stand covered with a tea towel for 5 minutes. Serve risotto with shaved parmesan.

*See Cooking Notes, p 38

CHEF'S TIP Steam or microwave 150g peeled, seeded butternut pumpkin until soft. Mash well with a fork or purée with a stick blender until smooth. Add 10g butter and season.
MIX & MATCH Add cooked, chopped Italian pork and veal sausages to the risotto during the last 5 minutes of cooking.

spaghetti with pesto

Serves: 4
Preparation: 15 mins
Cooking: 15 mins

400g spaghetti
Olive oil, to drizzle
Basil leaves, to serve

Pesto
60g pine nuts, roasted*
160g (2 cups firmly packed)
  basil leaves
60g (¾ cup) grated
  parmesan*
3 cloves garlic,
  roughly chopped
250ml (1 cup) olive oil
1 tbs lemon juice

1 To make pesto, process pine nuts, basil, parmesan and garlic in a food processor until finely chopped. Pour the oil into a jug and, with the motor running, gradually add oil in a thin stream and process until mixture is combined and smooth. Add lemon juice. Transfer to a bowl and season. Makes 1½ cups.

2 Meanwhile, cook pasta in a large saucepan of boiling salted water according to the packet instructions or until al dente (see Cooking Notes, p 38). Drain in a colander.

3 Drizzle a little olive oil into the same saucepan and add pasta. Stir in ½ cup pesto and mix well. Divide pasta among 4 bowls, top each with 1 tablespoon of pesto and scatter with basil leaves. Serve immediately.

*See Cooking Notes, p 38

MIX & MATCH Any remaining pesto can be stored in a screw-top jar. Cover with a thin layer of olive oil and refrigerate for up to 5 days. Pesto can be added to pizzas, salads and sandwiches. Alternatively, use toasted almonds instead of pine nuts and a mixture of parsley and basil leaves.

CHEF'S TIP

Adding oil to your saucepan of boiling water is a waste, as it just gets drained down the sink at the end. And don't rinse the cooked pasta under hot water, as it will remove those lovely starches that your pesto or sauce stick to.

eggplant parmigiana

Serves: 4
Preparation: 15 mins
Cooking: 45 mins

3 small eggplants
120g (1½ cups)
    grated parmesan
200g cherry bocconcini*,
    roughly chopped
140g (2 cups) fresh
    breadcrumbs*

Tomato sauce
60ml (¼ cup) olive oil
1 onion, finely chopped
4 cloves garlic,
    finely chopped
2 tsp chopped oregano
2 x 400g cans chopped
    tomatoes
½ cup loosely packed
    basil leaves, torn
    (see Chef's Tip)

1 To make tomato sauce, heat oil in a saucepan over medium heat, add onion and garlic and cook, stirring occasionally, for 5 minutes or until softened. Stir in oregano and cook for a further 2 minutes or until onion is light golden. Add tomatoes, season with salt and pepper and bring to the boil. Reduce heat to low, cover with a lid and simmer for 15 minutes. Stir in torn basil.

2 Meanwhile, cut eggplants into 5mm-thick rounds. Heat a chargrill pan or barbecue over high heat. Grill eggplant, in batches, for 2 minutes on each side or until lightly charred. Transfer to a bowl and cover with a tea towel. Repeat with remaining eggplant.

3 Preheat oven to 190C. Lightly oil a 1.5 litre (6-cup) ovenproof dish. Place a layer of eggplant in the bottom and spoon one-third of sauce over. Scatter with one-third of parmesan and bocconcini. Top with a second layer of eggplant, then spoon over half the remaining sauce and cheeses. Finish with final layer of eggplant and top with remaining sauce. Mix remaining cheeses with breadcrumbs and scatter over sauce. Bake for 30 minutes or until top is golden. Stand for 5 minutes before serving.

*See Cooking Notes, p 38

CHEF'S TIP Tear the basil leaves just before they are added to the sauce to prevent the leaves oxidising and going black.
MIX & MATCH Replace eggplant with chargrilled zucchini for a change.

lemon sorbetto

Serves: 4

Preparation: 20 mins
+ 9 hrs freezing time

Cooking: 5 mins

220g (1 cup) caster sugar
250ml (1 cup) strained
    lemon juice
1 tbs finely grated
    lemon zest
2 tbs mascarpone
Raspberries, to serve

1 Combine sugar and 200ml water in a small saucepan and stir over low heat until sugar has dissolved. Using a wet pastry brush, brush any crystals from side of pan. Bring to the boil, then turn heat to low and simmer, without stirring, for 5 minutes.

2 Transfer to a bowl and stir in lemon juice and zest. Cool completely before whisking in the mascarpone. Pour mixture into a shallow 18cm round cake pan and freeze for 6 hours.

3 Remove sorbetto from the freezer and blend in a food processor to break up the ice crystals that may have formed. Return to the freezer for 3 hours or until firm. Serve scoops of sorbetto with raspberries.

MIX & MATCH Reserve 4 lemon halves after juicing and use them to serve sorbetto. To prepare, using the tip of a dessertspoon, scrape away the pith and any remaining flesh, taking care not to pierce the skin. Trim bottom of lemon halves so they sit flat. Refrigerate until ready to fill.

cassata cake

Serves: 6–8

Preparation: 30 mins
+ 3 hrs refrigeration

600g (2½ cups)
 fresh ricotta (see
 Cooking Notes, p 38)
80g icing sugar, plus extra,
 to sift
½ tsp finely grated
 orange zest
200g mixed glacé fruit,
 roughly chopped
 (see Chef's Tips)
50g dark chocolate
 (70% cocoa solids),
 finely grated, plus extra,
 to sprinkle
500g sponge cake
125ml (½ cup) freshly
 squeezed orange juice
1 orange, peeled,
 segmented, to serve

1 Line base of a 20cm springform pan with baking paper. Process ricotta and icing sugar in a food processor until smooth. Transfer to a bowl and stir in orange zest. Fold in glacé fruit and grated chocolate. Cover with plastic wrap and refrigerate until ready to use.

2 Slice sponge horizontally into 5mm-thick slices. Place a disc of sponge into prepared cake pan, then cut more sponge to line the inside, trimming to fit (see Cooking Notes, p 38). Set aside remaining slices of sponge. Using a pastry brush, brush three-quarters of the orange juice generously over base and side of sponge in pan.

3 Spoon ricotta mixture into sponge lining and smooth top. Cover top with remaining sponge (there may be slices left over) and brush with remaining juice. Refrigerate for at least 3 hours.

4 Release springform pan, then invert cake onto a large plate. Sift icing sugar over cake and sprinkle with a little extra grated chocolate. Serve slices of cassata with segmented orange.

CHEF'S TIPS Instead of using a springform cake pan, use a base-lined 2 litre (8-cup) pudding basin. Any leftover cake can be frozen and later used in a trifle.
SHOPPING LIST Glacé fruit, such as peaches, apricots, pineapple and pears, are available from health food shops, delis and specialist food shops.

GREECE

PUMPKIN FILO PIE

*

STUFFED PEPPERS
AND ZUCCHINIS

*

PASTITSO

*

SOUVLAKIA WITH
PITA BREAD

*

GREEK LAMB WITH
LEMON POTATOES

*

BAKED CHICKEN
WITH ORZO

*

SEMOLINA SYRUP CAKE

Γειά σου
καλή όρεξη!

'Cheers,
eat well!'

Thessaloniki

Athens

Samos

Santorini

GREECE   Crete

GREECE COOKING NOTES

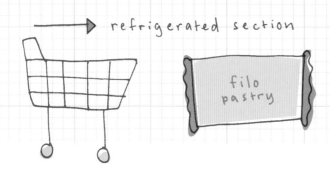

refrigerated section

filo pastry

Filo pastry

Filo pastry is available from the refrigerated and frozen sections of supermarkets. For the pumpkin filo pie recipe (page 58) and other whole savoury pies, it's best to use the refrigerated variety because it will give the pie a slightly thicker and crunchier crust when cooked.

If you use thawed frozen filo for the pumpkin pie recipe, use a total of 12 sheets – 9 on the base and 3 cut in half for the top. When working with any filo, keep the sheets covered with a clean, slightly damp tea towel to prevent it drying out (for more on filo, see Moroccan Cooking Notes, page 158).

DRIED GREEK OREGANO

Dried Greek oregano (*rigani*) is available packed in bunches, with flowers attached, from delis and greengrocers. It has a stronger flavour and scent than when you pick it fresh.

KEFALOGRAVIERA This is a hard, salty, sheep's milk cheese available from delis, specialist food shops and selected supermarkets. Kefalotiri is another hard cheese made from sheep's or goat's milk. If you can't find them, you can substitute either of these with pecorino romano or parmesan.

GREEK VILLAGE SALAD

Cut 1 tomato and ½ red onion into wedges. Place into a bowl with ½ chopped red capsicum, 1 sliced Lebanese cucumber and 30g Kalamata olives. Pour 2 tbs extra virgin olive oil and 2 tsp red wine vinegar into a small jar with a lid and season. Shake well and pour over salad. Toss to combine. Place a 100g piece of Greek feta cheese on top and sprinkle with ½ tsp dried Greek oregano.

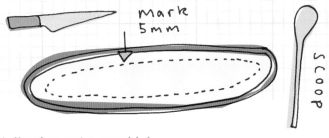

Mark 5mm

scoop

Hollowing out a zucchini

For stuffed peppers and zucchinis (page 60), turn zucchini on its side and, using a small, sharp knife, cut down the length 1cm from the edge to cut off the top. Turn the zucchini back on its base. Using a small teaspoon, scoop out the flesh and reserve, leaving a 5mm shell. A food processor fitted with the cutting attachment can be used to chop up the onion and then the pepper and zucchini flesh.

pumpkin filo pie

Serves: 6
***
Preparation: 40 mins
+ 10 mins cooling time
***
Cooking: 1 hr
***

500g jap pumpkin, peeled,
   seeded, cut into large
   chunks (get an adult to
   help you)
100g fresh ricotta
150g (¾ cup) Greek
   feta, crumbled
2 tbs short-grain rice
1 tbs olive oil
2 eggs
1 tbs honey
¼ tsp ground cinnamon
Pinch ground nutmeg
90g unsalted butter, melted
11 sheets filo pastry*
Greek village salad*,
   to serve

CHEF'S TIP When scoring
pastry, make sure you
don't cut all the way
through to the filling. The
score marks will help you
cut the pie cleanly when
serving. For a crisp top,
just before baking, spray
pastry lightly with water
by wetting your hand
then shaking it over pie.

1 Preheat oven to 180C. Place pumpkin in a food processor and process in short bursts until roughly chopped. Transfer pumpkin to a bowl. Add ricotta, feta, rice, oil, eggs, honey and spices. Season with salt and pepper, and stir with a large spoon until just combined.

2 Brush a 20cm square cake pan with melted butter. Brush 1 sheet filo with butter and line the base and sides of the prepared pan, allowing excess to overhang rim. Brush another sheet with butter and place on top. Continue layering until there are 8 sheets lining the base of the prepared pan.

3 Spoon in the pumpkin filling. Cut the remaining 3 sheets of filo in half. Brush 1 sheet of filo with butter and place over filling. Continue layering until all remaining sheets of filo are used. Brush top with butter. Trim excess pastry, leaving 2cm overhanging, then fold this over to seal edges around the pan. Using a sharp knife, score top into squares (see Chef's Tip), then pierce the top layers down to the filling in two or three places to allow the steam to escape. Bake pie for 40 minutes, check pie (cover with foil if it's over-browning), then cook for a further 20 minutes or until golden and well risen.

4 Turn out onto a wire rack and cool for 10 minutes before turning it back into the pan and cutting pie (this helps keep its shape). Serve at room temperature with a Greek salad.

*See Cooking Notes, p 56

stuffed peppers and zucchinis

Serves: 4

Preparation: 30 mins

Cooking: 1 hr 20 mins

4 (300g) red banana
   peppers or small
   red capsicum
4 (480g) zucchinis
60ml (¼ cup) olive oil
1 onion, chopped
65g (⅓ cup) short-grain rice
250ml (1 cup) vegetable or
   chicken stock
1 tbs tomato paste
¼ tsp ground cinnamon
1 tbs chopped flat-leaf
   parsley
1 tbs chopped mint
1 tbs currants
8 cherry tomatoes,
   thinly sliced

1 Preheat oven to 180C. Place a pepper on its side on a chopping board. Cut down the side to expose the cavity, then cut the top off the pepper and reserve. Turn pepper back on its base and pull out seeds and membrane. Repeat with remaining peppers.

2 Place a zucchini on its side on a chopping board, cut the top off lengthwise, then scoop out flesh to form a cavity. Reserve flesh (see Cooking Notes, p 56). Repeat with remaining zucchinis.

3 Heat 1 tbs oil in a frying pan over medium heat. Add onion and cook, stirring, over low–medium heat for 5 minutes or until onion is softened. Add rice and cook, stirring, for 2 minutes. Stir in reserved peppers and zucchini flesh, stock, tomato paste and cinnamon. Increase heat to high, bring to the boil, then reduce heat to medium and simmer for 5 minutes. Remove from the heat and stir in parsley, mint and currants. Season with salt and pepper.

4 Using a teaspoon, spoon rice mixture into the peppers and zucchini shells. Place stuffed vegetables in an oiled ovenproof dish that will comfortably fit the peppers and zucchinis in a single layer. Drizzle vegetables with any pan juices, then place tomato slices on top. Drizzle with remaining 2 tbs olive oil. Pour 2 tbs water in dish around vegetables and season. Cover loosely with foil and bake for 30 minutes. Remove foil and bake for a further 40 minutes or until rice and vegetables are tender.

pastitso

Serves: 6
Preparation: 40 mins
Cooking: 1 hr 25 mins

250g tortiglioni pasta
  or penne
40g (½ cup) finely grated
  kefalograviera*
¼ tsp ground nutmeg
2 tsp dried packaged
  breadcrumbs
Baby cos and cherry tomato
  salad, to serve

Meat sauce
1 tbs olive oil
20g butter
1 large onion, chopped
500g minced beef (see
  Chef's Tip)
500ml (2 cups) passata
  (sieved puréed tomatoes)
250ml (1 cup) chicken stock
  or water
½ tsp ground cinnamon
¼ tsp ground cloves
1 bay leaf

Ricotta topping
500g fresh ricotta
80g finely grated
  kefalograviera*
2 eggs
Pinch ground nutmeg

1 To make meat sauce, heat oil and butter in a large, heavy-based saucepan over medium heat. Add onion and cook, stirring, for 5 minutes or until softened. Increase heat to high, add mince and cook, stirring, breaking up the mince with a wooden spoon, for 5 minutes or until browned and liquid has evaporated. Stir in passata, stock, cinnamon, cloves and bay leaf, and bring to the boil. Reduce heat to low and simmer, stirring occasionally, for 30 minutes or until thick. Season with ½ tsp sugar and salt and pepper.

2 Meanwhile, preheat oven to 180C. Grease a 2.5-litre (10-cup) ovenproof dish. To make ricotta topping, place ricotta, kefalograviera, eggs and nutmeg in a food processor. Season with salt and pepper, then process until smooth.

3 Cook pasta in a large saucepan of boiling salted water according to packet directions or until al dente (see Italian Cooking Notes, p 38). Drain in a colander. Spoon half the pasta into prepared dish. Sprinkle with 2 tbs of kefalograviera, then spoon the meat sauce over. Top with the remaining pasta and 3½ tbs of the remaining kefalograviera. Spoon ricotta topping over and spread evenly. Sprinkle with remaining kefalograviera, nutmeg and breadcrumbs. Bake for 45 minutes or until golden and bubbling. Stand for 5 minutes, then serve with salad.

*See Cooking Notes, p 56

CHEF'S TIP When browning any meat, remove it from the fridge 1 hour before cooking to bring it to room temperature. It will brown better and not stew in the pan. TIME SAVER Meat sauce can be made up to 2 days ahead and stored, covered, in the refrigerator. It doesn't need to be reheated to assemble the pastitso.

souvlakia with pita bread

Serves: 4
Preparation: 30 mins
Cooking: 15 mins

2 tsp dried Greek oregano
   (see Cooking Notes, p 56)
½ tsp paprika
½ tsp grated lemon zest
80ml (⅓ cup) lemon juice,
   plus 1 tbs extra
1 clove garlic, crushed
500g diced lean pork leg
   or shoulder
6 bamboo skewers, soaked
   in water for 30 minutes,
   drained (see Australian
   Cooking Notes, p 6)
1 tbs olive oil
4 pita breads
2 tbs chopped mint

Tzatziki
½ Lebanese cucumber
140g (½ cup) Greek-style
   yoghurt
2 cloves garlic, crushed
2 tsp red wine vinegar
1 tbs olive oil

1 To make tzatziki, coarsely grate cucumber into a bowl. Season with ½ tsp salt and set aside for 5 minutes. Place in a colander and drain, pressing down to remove excess liquid, then return cucumber to bowl. Stir in yoghurt, garlic, vinegar and olive oil, then season with salt and pepper. Cover with plastic wrap and refrigerate until needed.

2 Combine oregano, paprika, lemon zest and juice, and garlic with ½ tsp black pepper in a bowl. Add pork and toss to combine. Thread the pork onto skewers. Heat a lightly oiled barbecue or chargrill until hot. Cook souvlakia for 10 minutes, turning occasionally, or until browned and cooked through.

3 Transfer skewers to a shallow dish. Whisk extra lemon juice with oil in a jug until combined, then season with salt and pepper. Drizzle over souvlakia, then cover loosely with foil.

4 Cook pita breads on a hotplate for 30 seconds each side or until soft. Smear tzatziki onto each bread. Carefully slide meat from skewers and place on top of tzatziki. Scatter with mint, then roll up bread tightly to serve.

greek lamb
with lemon potatoes

Serves: 6

Preparation: 15 mins

Cooking: 2 hrs

1.5kg leg lamb
  (see Chef's Tip)
3 cloves garlic, halved
3 lemons, juiced
3 tsp dried Greek oregano
  (see Cooking Notes, p 56)
750g coliban or sebago
  potatoes (see English
  Cooking Notes, p 108)
2 tbs olive oil

1 Preheat oven to 160C. Using the tip of a small, sharp knife, cut 6 incisions all over lamb, each large enough to hold a piece of garlic. Push a piece of garlic into each incision. Place lamb in a large roasting pan. Pour half the lemon juice over lamb, sprinkle with half the oregano and season with salt and pepper.

2 Peel and cut each potato lengthwise into 6 wedges. Place in a bowl and add remaining lemon juice, and oregano and oil. Season and toss to coat. Place around lamb in roasting pan and cover with foil. Roast for 1 hour 20 minutes (see Chef's Tip). Remove foil, increase heat to 230C and roast for a further 30 minutes or until lamb is medium to well done when tested.

3 Transfer lamb to a plate. Cover with foil and rest while finishing potatoes. Using a slotted spoon, transfer potatoes to a plate. Carefully pour pan juices from pan into a jug. Use a spoon to skim off fat. Return juices to pan, add potatoes, turn to coat in juices, then return to oven for 10 minutes or until golden. Serve lemon potatoes with sliced lamb.

CHEF'S TIP Remove lamb from fridge 1 hour prior to cooking to bring it to room temperature. If lamb is taken directly from the fridge, roast for a further 10 minutes. To test if lamb is done, insert a skewer into the thickest part of the lamb. For rare, the juices will be red, for medium, the juices should be pink and for well done, the juices should be clear.

baked chicken with orzo

Serves: 4
Preparation: 10 mins
Cooking: 1 hr 15 mins

3 chicken drumsticks
3 chicken thigh cutlets
10g butter
2 tsp olive oil
375ml (1½ cups)
   chicken stock
400g can chopped
   tomatoes
¼ tsp ground cinnamon
200g orzo pasta
   (see Chef's Tips)
90g finely grated
   kefalograviera (see
   Cooking Notes, p 56)

1 Preheat oven to 180C. Season chicken with salt and pepper. Heat butter and oil in a large, non-stick frying pan over high heat and brown chicken, in 2 batches, for 3 minutes each side or until browned all over (see Chef's Tips). Transfer to a plate.

2 Pour stock and half the tomatoes into the same pan and bring to the boil, stirring, scraping any brown pieces from the base of the pan. Add cinnamon and pasta, and season. Pour mixture into a 2-litre (8-cup) ovenproof dish that will fit chicken pieces in a single layer (this will ensure that the pasta cooks evenly). Arrange chicken over top, then pour remaining tomatoes over chicken. Cover with foil and bake for 45 minutes. Remove foil and scatter with kefalograviera. Bake, uncovered, for a further 15 minutes or until pasta is tender and cheese is melted and golden.

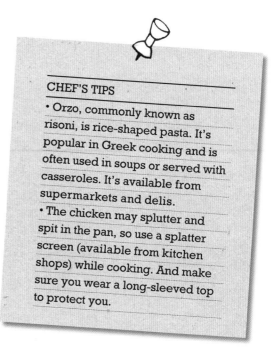

CHEF'S TIPS
• Orzo, commonly known as risoni, is rice-shaped pasta. It's popular in Greek cooking and is often used in soups or served with casseroles. It's available from supermarkets and delis.
• The chicken may splutter and spit in the pan, so use a splatter screen (available from kitchen shops) while cooking. And make sure you wear a long-sleeved top to protect you.

semolina syrup cake

Makes: 20 pieces

Preparation: 15 mins
+ 3 hrs cooling time

Cooking: 30 mins

85g blanched almonds

75g (½ cup) self-raising flour

¼ tsp baking powder

125g unsalted butter,
  softened, chopped

110g (½ cup) caster sugar

1 tsp finely grated
  lemon zest

3 eggs, at room
  temperature

160g (1 cup) semolina (see
  Cooking Notes, p 56)

Syrup

440g (2 cups) caster sugar

1 tbs lemon juice

1 Preheat oven to 180C. Grease and line the base of a 20cm square cake pan with baking paper. Process 40g almonds in a food processor until coarsely ground. Sift flour and baking powder into a bowl. Using an electric mixer, beat butter, sugar and zest for 6 minutes or until pale and fluffy. Add eggs, one at a time, beating well after each addition. Using a large metal spoon, fold in ground almonds, sifted flour mixture and semolina. Spoon mixture into prepared cake pan and smooth top. Bake for 25 minutes or until a skewer inserted into the centre comes out clean. Place cake in pan on a wire rack.

2 Meanwhile, to make syrup, combine sugar, lemon juice and 375ml (1½ cups) water in a saucepan over low heat, stirring until sugar dissolves. Increase heat to medium, bring to the boil, and boil for 3 minutes until slightly reduced (see Chef's Tip).

3 Spoon two-thirds of the hot syrup evenly over warm cake in pan, then set aside for 3 hours to cool and for syrup to be absorbed. Cut cake into 5cm squares and place one remaining almond in the centre of each square. Drizzle over a little of the remaining syrup to serve.

MORE PLEASE

Store cake in the tin it is baked in, as the syrup helps to preserve it and keep it moist. It will keep well, covered with foil, for up to 5 days. In warmer months, refrigerate for up to 1 week and remove from the fridge 1 hour before serving.

CHEF'S TIP To prevent the syrup from crystallising, always dissolve the sugar in the water before syrup begins to boil. Then, use a pastry brush dipped in water to brush down the side of the pan and remove any sugar crystals.

CHINa

SALT AND PEPPER
CALAMARI

*

PRAWN AND PORK SIU MAI

*

FRIED RICE WITH
PRAWNS AND EGG

*

BEEF AND BLACK
BEAN STIR-FRY

*

CHICKEN, CASHEW AND
SUGAR SNAP STIR-FRY

*

CHAR SIU PORK
WITH STIR-FRIED
ASIAN GREENS

*

CHINESE BOLOGNESE

Beijing.

CHINA

Shanghai.

. Hong Kong

Yum cha means
'tasting of tea'

CHINA COOKING NOTES

Tips for stir-frying

This is a technique where you need to be really organised beforehand, as cooking should be done quickly. Make sure you prepare all the ingredients beforehand – this is known as *mise en place* (pronounced 'meez on plass'), literally 'put in place'. Cut all the ingredients into pieces about the same size so they cook evenly. The dish will look and taste much better.

SOYBEAN FLAVOURINGS*

Salted black beans are soybeans that have been dried and fermented with salt.

Salted soy beans are made from yellow soy beans, and can be substituted with yellow bean sauce/paste from supermarkets.

* Both these ingredients are available from Asian grocers.

yellow bean paste

fermented black beans

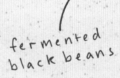

DUMPLING WRAPPERS These are square, and are made from flour, eggs and water. They're available from Asian grocers both in the frozen and refrigerated sections, and in selected supermarkets.

oyster
sauce

light
soy sauce

shaoxing

sesame
oil

Season to taste*

Oyster sauce A thick, salty sauce originally made by reducing the broth from cooking oysters; these days, cornflour and caramel are usually added to reduce the cost.

Light soy sauce Saltier and less thick than soy sauce. Soy sauce is made with soybeans and roasted wheat fermented with salt and yeast, then aged before bottling.

Shaoxing This rice wine is named after the town in Northern China that's been producing it for more than 2000 years.

Sesame oil Dark, roasted sesame oil is commonly used in Chinese cooking. Use it sparingly as it has a strong flavour.

* All available from Asian grocers and selected supermarkets.

SZECHUAN PEPPER Also used in five-spice mix, this is not a pepper, but the dried seed shells of a prickly ash tree. Its unique clove/citrus flavour has a 'numbing' effect on the mouth, and is said to offset the heat of chilli.

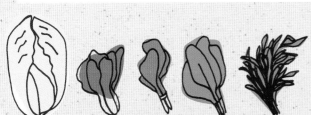

Wombok

Bok choy

Gai lan

Choy sum

Kang kong

ASIAN GREENS
- Wombok (Chinese cabbage)
- Bok choy (also sold as pak choy)
- Gai lan (Chinese broccoli)
- Choy sum (or flowering choy sum)
- Kang kong (water spinach or water convolvulus)

salt and pepper calamari

Serves: 4

Preparation: 10 mins
+ 30 mins marinating time

Cooking: 8 mins

450g calamari tubes
    (see Shopping List)
2 tbs fish sauce
2 tsp caster sugar
75g (½ cup)
    self-raising flour
60ml (¼ cup) vegetable oil
150g (1 cup) cornflour
Vegetable oil, to deep-fry
    (See Mexican Cooking
    Notes, p 190)

Szechuan salt and pepper
1 tsp Szechuan pepper*
3 tsp salt

SHOPPING LIST
Calamari tubes are
available from selected
supermarkets and
fishmongers.

1 To prepare calamari, slice down the length of one side of the tubes, open out and place them flat on a chopping board. Cut tubes widthwise into 1cm-thick strips. Transfer to a bowl, add fish sauce and sugar, and stir to combine. Cover and marinate in the fridge for 30 minutes.

2 To make Szechuan salt and pepper, heat a wok over medium heat, add Szechuan pepper and salt, and stir-fry for 30 seconds or until pepper begins to pop. Using a mortar and pestle (see Thai Cooking Notes, p 172), grind to a fine powder.

3 Combine flour, oil and 80ml (⅓ cup) water in a bowl and stir to form a very thick batter. Place cornflour in a separate bowl. Working in batches, dip calamari in batter and coat evenly, then shake off excess. Add to cornflour, toss to coat, then shake off excess. Place in a clean bowl. Repeat with remaining calamari, batter and cornflour, adding more cornflour to the bowl if necessary (don't worry if batter becomes lumpy).

4 Fill a deep-fryer or large saucepan one-third full with oil (get an adult to help you) and heat over medium heat to 180C. (To check oil is sufficiently hot, add a 1.5cm cube of bread to pan – if it turns golden in 35 seconds, the oil is ready.) Increase heat to high. Using tongs, place half the calamari in oil and fry for 30 seconds, moving pieces around to break up any that have stuck together. Fry for a further 2 minutes or until crisp and golden. Remove with a slotted spoon and drain on paper towel. Repeat with remaining calamari. Serve with Szechuan salt and pepper.

*See Cooking Notes, p 74

prawn and pork siu mai

Makes: 26
Preparation: 35 mins
Cooking: 6 mins

500g green king prawns,
   peeled, cleaned, roughly
   chopped* (see Australian
   Cooking Notes, p 6)
4 spring onions, sliced
3cm piece ginger, grated
½ tsp sesame oil*
1½ tbs light soy sauce*
2 tsp caster sugar
150g minced pork
Vegetable oil, to brush
26 fresh dumpling
   wrappers* (see Chef's Tip)

Soy ginger dipping sauce
80ml (⅓ cup)
   light soy sauce*
2 tbs rice vinegar*
1 tbs caster sugar
2 tsp sesame oil*
2cm piece ginger, grated
2 tsp chopped coriander

1 To make soy ginger dipping sauce, combine soy sauce, rice vinegar, sugar, sesame oil and ginger in a bowl and whisk until sugar has dissolved. Add coriander just before serving.

2 Combine prawns, spring onions, ginger, sesame oil, soy sauce, sugar, ½ tsp salt and ¼ tsp pepper in a food processor and process until smooth. Add pork and process until just combined. Transfer to a bowl.

3 Brush base of a bamboo steamer (see Shopping List) with oil. Working in batches (see Chef's Tip), place 4 dumpling wrappers on a clean work surface and place 1 tbs of mixture in centre of each. Gather up sides of each wrapper and mould it around mixture, leaving top open and pressing base on bench to flatten it. Place dumplings in steamer, 2cm apart. Repeat with remaining dumpling wrappers and mixture. Cover steamer and place over a saucepan of simmering water. Steam dumplings for 6 minutes or until cooked through. Serve with soy ginger dipping sauce.

*See Cooking Notes, p 74

CHEF'S TIP Fresh dumpling wrappers dry out very quickly when left uncovered, making them crack, tear and difficult to mould. Only work with a small number at a time, leaving the remainder covered with plastic wrap or a slightly damp tea towel.

SHOPPING LIST
Bamboo steamers are available at selected Asian supermarkets and grocers. They come in a variety of sizes.

fried rice with prawns and egg

Serves: 4
Preparation: 20 mins
Cooking: 10 mins

460g (3 cups) cooked
  medium-grain rice, chilled
  (see Chef's Tip)
2 tbs light soy sauce*
1 small carrot, chopped
60g (½ cup) frozen peas
300g green king prawns,
  peeled, cleaned, roughly
  chopped (see Australian
  Cooking Notes, p 6)
2 tbs vegetable oil
1 tsp sesame oil*
2 eggs, lightly beaten
4 cloves garlic,
  finely chopped
3cm piece ginger,
  finely chopped
4 spring onions, sliced

1 Place rice in a bowl, add soy sauce and a pinch each of salt and sugar. Using a fork, fluff up rice well, breaking up any lumps. Set aside.

2 Blanch carrot in a saucepan of boiling water for 1 minute. Add peas and cook for a further 20 seconds. Drain in a colander and refresh in iced water, then drain again.

3 Season prawns with a pinch each of salt and sugar. Heat a wok over high heat, add 2 tsp vegetable oil and ½ tsp sesame oil and stir-fry prawns for 30 seconds. Pour in eggs and stir for 20 seconds or until eggs are just cooked but still very soft. Transfer to a plate and set aside. Wipe wok clean.

4 Place wok over medium heat and add remaining oils. When smoking, add garlic and ginger, and stir-fry for 15 seconds. Increase heat to high, add rice and cook for 2 minutes, stirring rapidly to move the rice around the wok. Add carrot and peas, and stir-fry for a further 2 minutes. Add prawn and egg mixture, and spring onions, then season with salt and pepper. Stir-fry for a further 1 minute, breaking up the egg and prawn mixture with a spoon. Transfer to bowls and serve immediately.

*See Cooking Notes, p 74

CHEF'S TIP For best results, use rice cooked the day before, which has been kept overnight in the fridge.

MIX AND MATCH Add leftover cooked meats such as sliced char siu pork or roast chicken to rice in addition to, or instead of, the prawns. Substitute carrots and peas with sliced beans, corn kernels or bok choy.

beef and black bean stir-fry

Serves: 4
Preparation: 10 mins
+ 30 mins marinating time
Cooking: 8 mins

1½ tbs light soy sauce
2 tsp caster sugar
2 tsp cornflour
400g beef sirloin or
   rump steak, trimmed
   of fat, thinly sliced
1 bunch gai lan*
   (Chinese broccoli)
80ml (⅓ cup) vegetable oil
1 small red onion, chopped
4 cloves garlic,
   finely chopped
3cm piece ginger,
   finely chopped
1 red capsicum, seeded,
   thinly sliced
100g oyster mushrooms,
   roughly torn if large
   (see Shopping List)
1 tbs salted black beans*
2 tbs Chinese rice wine
   (shaoxing)*
2 tbs oyster sauce*

1 Combine soy sauce, sugar and cornflour in a bowl, add beef and toss to combine. Cover and marinate in the fridge for 30 minutes.

2 Cut gai lan leaves from stems and trim base of stems. Slice remaining stems lengthwise if thick, then cut leaves into 5cm lengths. Set aside separately.

3 Heat a wok over high heat and add 1½ tbs oil. When very hot, add half the beef and stir-fry (see Cooking Notes, p 74) over high heat for 2 minutes or until beef is browned. Transfer beef to a bowl and repeat with another 1½ tbs oil and remaining beef. Wipe wok clean.

4 Place wok over medium heat. When hot, add remaining 1 tbs oil, then onion, garlic and ginger. Stir-fry for 1 minute. Increase heat to high, add gai lan stems, capsicum and mushrooms and stir-fry for 2 minutes. Add gai lan leaves, black beans and rice wine, and stir-fry for 30 seconds. Return beef to wok, add oyster sauce and 60ml (¼ cup) water and stir-fry for a further 30 seconds. Serve immediately.

*See Cooking Notes, p 74

SHOPPING LIST Oyster mushrooms are available at supermarkets. Substitute with Swiss brown or shiitake mushrooms if they are unavailable.

chicken, cashew and sugar snap stir-fry

Serves: 4

Preparation: 10 mins
+ 30 mins marinating time

Cooking: 4 mins

1 tbs light soy sauce*

1 tbs Chinese rice
   wine (shaoxing)*

1 tbs caster sugar

60ml (¼ cup) vegetable oil

2 tsp cornflour

400g chicken thigh fillets,
   trimmed of fat, cut into
   2cm pieces

2 bok choy*

3cm piece ginger, peeled,
   finely sliced

150g sugar snap peas,
   trimmed

40g roasted
   unsalted cashews
   (see Chef's Tip)

Steamed rice,
   to serve

1 Combine soy sauce, rice wine, sugar and 1 tbs vegetable oil in a bowl. Whisk to dissolve sugar, then add cornflour and stir until smooth. Add chicken and toss to combine, then cover and marinate in the fridge for 30 minutes.

2 Cut bok choy leaves from stems and trim base of stems, then cut leaves into 5cm lengths. Set aside.

3 Heat a wok over high heat. Add 1 tbs oil, then add chicken. Spread chicken around wok and cook for 1 minute, without stirring, or until starting to brown on the bottom, then stir-fry for a further 1 minute. Transfer to a plate. Wipe wok clean.

4 Heat wok over high heat. Add remaining 1 tbs oil, then add ginger and sugar snap peas, and stir-fry for 30 seconds. Add bok choy and 1 tsp salt, and stir-fry for a further 30 seconds. Return chicken to wok, add 60ml (¼ cup) water and stir-fry for a further 30 seconds. Add cashews and toss to combine. Serve immediately with steamed rice.

*See Cooking Notes, p 74

CHEF'S TIP

If roasted unsalted cashews are unavailable, place raw cashews on an oven tray and roast at 180C for 4–5 minutes or until golden.

MIX AND MATCH If Chinese rice wine (shaoxing) is unavailable, substitute with dry sherry.

char siu pork with stir-fried asian greens

Serves: 4
Preparation: 15 mins
+ 2 hrs marinating time
Cooking: 40 mins

500g pork scotch fillet
  (neck), cut lengthwise
  into 4cm-wide strips
120g (⅓ cup) char siu sauce
  (see Shopping List)
90g (¼ cup) honey, to brush

Stir-fried Asian greens
1 tbs vegetable oil
3 cloves garlic,
  finely chopped
5 shiitake or button
  mushrooms, stems
  removed, sliced
4 bok choy*, each cut into
  6 lengthwise
100g snow peas, trimmed
1½ tbs oyster sauce*

1 Place pork strips in a bowl and coat well with char siu sauce. Cover and marinate in fridge for 2 hours.

2 Preheat oven to 180C. Line a roasting pan with foil, then place a wire rack in pan. Place pork on rack, reserving any marinade in bowl. Roast pork for 15 minutes. Increase oven temperature to 220C, remove pork and brush with marinade to baste. Turn pork over and roast for a further 15 minutes. Brush honey over pork and cook for a further 3 minutes or until pork is cooked through. Rest for 5 minutes, then slice thickly.

3 To make stir-fried Asian greens, heat a wok over high heat. When hot, add oil and garlic, and stir-fry for 15 seconds. Add mushrooms and stir-fry for 30 seconds, add bok choy and stir-fry for 2 minutes, then add snow peas and stir-fry for a further 30 seconds. Add oyster sauce, a pinch of salt and 60ml (¼ cup) water and toss for 30 seconds or until combined and warmed through. Serve immediately with sliced char siu pork.

*See Cooking Notes, p 74

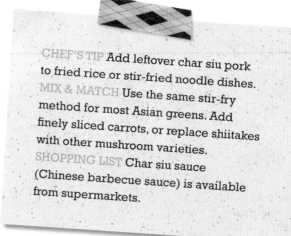

CHEF'S TIP Add leftover char siu pork to fried rice or stir-fried noodle dishes.
MIX & MATCH Use the same stir-fry method for most Asian greens. Add finely sliced carrots, or replace shiitakes with other mushroom varieties.
SHOPPING LIST Char siu sauce (Chinese barbecue sauce) is available from supermarkets.

chinese bolognese

Serves: 4
Preparation: 20 mins
Cooking: 15 mins

500g minced pork
80ml (⅓ cup) light
   soy sauce*
4 cloves garlic,
   roughly chopped
5cm piece ginger,
   roughly chopped
8 spring onions, sliced,
   plus extra, thinly sliced
   lengthwise, to serve
2 tbs tahini (See Moroccan
   Cooking Notes, p 158)
2 tbs salted soybeans*
50g (¼ cup) caster sugar
375ml (1½ cups)
   chicken stock
60ml (¼ cup) vegetable oil
½ tsp sesame oil*
400g fresh Chinese wheat
   flour noodles (see
   Shopping List)
1 Lebanese cucumber,
   seeded, thinly peeled
   into ribbons

1 Place pork and 2 tbs soy sauce in a bowl and stir to combine. Cover with plastic wrap and refrigerate until needed.

2 Using a mortar and pestle (see Thai Cooking Notes, p 172), pound garlic, ginger and a pinch of salt to a fine paste. Add spring onions and pound to a coarse paste. (If you don't have a mortar and pestle, finely chop garlic and ginger and combine with spring onions and a pinch of salt.)

3 Place tahini, salted soybeans, sugar, stock and remaining 2 tbs soy sauce in a bowl and whisk to combine.

4 Heat a wok over high heat and add half the vegetable oil. When oil is smoking add pork and stir-fry for 3 minutes or until browned, breaking up any lumps with a wooden spoon. Transfer to a bowl. Clean wok and place over medium heat. Add remaining vegetable oil and garlic mixture and stir-fry for 30 seconds. Increase heat to high, return pork to wok and add tahini mixture. Bring to the boil, then reduce heat and simmer for 10 minutes or until sauce has thickened and meat is tender. Remove from heat and stir in sesame oil.

5 Meanwhile, bring a large saucepan of salted water to the boil. Add noodles, return to the boil and cook according to packet instructions or until al dente (see Italian Cooking Notes, p 38). Drain. To serve, place noodles on a plate, spoon pork mixture over noodles, top with cucumber and sprinkle with extra spring onions.

*See Cooking Notes, p 74

SHOPPING LIST

Fresh Chinese wheat flour noodles are available from the refrigerated section of supermarkets and Asian grocers.

India's population is 1.2 billion. That's a lot of delicious curries to prepare!

INDIA

While some Indians do eat beef, the cow is sacred in Hinduism.

New Delhi

Kolkata

Mumbai

Chennai

INDIA

VEGETABLE BHAJI WITH MINT RAITA
*
CHICKEN WITH TOMATOES AND CURRY LEAVES
*
TIKKA LAMB CUTLETS WITH CORIANDER RAITA
*
CREAMY SPICED PRAWNS WITH BASMATI PILAU
*
INDIAN GRILLED FISH WITH CARROT AND CASHEW PACHADI
*
BEEF MADRAS CURRY

INDIA COOKING NOTES

RAITA

This Indian side dish can be flavoured with many different ingredients, but its base is always yoghurt. Yoghurt features a lot in Indian cooking, adding thickness and creaminess to curries, and helping to tenderise meats in marinades such as tandoori. Plus, it cools the mouth after too much spice! It's also made into a refreshing drink called lassi, which is flavoured with salt, or sweetened with sugar and fruit, such as mango or banana.

paratha   chapati   poori

naan   pappadum

Indian breads

Paratha Crisp, flaky pan-fried flatbread made from wholemeal flour (also known as roti).
Chapati A soft flatbread made with yoghurt.
Poori Crisp golden bread that puffs up to a ball when fried.
Naan Leavened (made with yeast) flatbread traditionally cooked in a tandoor (earthenware oven). Naan comes in many varieties of flavours including garlic.
Pappadum Thin, crisp fried wafers made from lentil flour. Moreish and easy to prepare, they are often served with raita.

DID YOU KNOW? There are many theories about where the word 'curry' comes from. The most popular one is that it's an English variation of a Tamil word *kari*, meaning 'spicy sauce', from the colonial days (1858-1947) when the British occupied India.

Spices (pictured from left to right)*

Cardamom Usually, the whole pod is 'bruised' (lightly crushed) before adding to a dish, then removed after cooking.

Black mustard seeds Used in many Indian dishes, particularly curries. They 'pop' as they're cooked, releasing a nutty aroma.

Garam masala A spice mix usually added at the end of cooking or just before serving so its fragrance is at its freshest.

Turmeric This vivid yellow spice is a member of the ginger family and has a mustard-like taste. Be careful handling it, as it stains!

Curry leaves Use fresh ones if possible, as they have the best flavour. They're sold in sprigs or in packs, and have a spicy aroma.

* All available from selected supermarkets, greengrocers and Indian food shops.

Tamarind purée

Made from pulp extracted from the pods of the tamarind tree, tamarind purée is widely used in Asian cooking for its sour flavour. You'll find it in jars at selected supermarkets and Asian food shops. Sometimes lemon or lime can be used as a substitute.

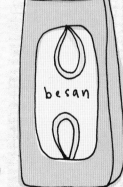

BESAN (CHICKPEA FLOUR)

Also known as gram or chana flour, besan is made from ground dried chickpeas. It is used widely in Indian, Pakistani and Bangladeshi cooking, as well as in parts of the Mediterranean. It is available from health food shops and the health food aisle of selected supermarkets, as well as Indian food shops.

vegetable bhaji with mint raita

Serves: 4

Preparation: 20 mins
+ 20 mins resting time

Cooking: 20 mins

225g (1½ cups) besan
   (chickpea) flour*
60g (⅓ cup) rice flour
½ tsp ground turmeric
¼ tsp chilli powder,
   (optional)
2 tbs vegetable oil
Vegetable oil, to deep-fry
   (see Chef's Tip)
4 spring onions, trimmed
   to 10cm
220g cauliflower, cut into
   1cm-thick slices
150g broccoli, cut into
   small florets
4 baby eggplants,
   quartered lengthwise
Tomato kasundi (see
   Shopping List) or tomato
   chutney, to serve

Mint raita
280g (1 cup) Greek-style
   yoghurt
½ cup chopped mint
2 tbs chopped coriander
1 tsp ginger, finely grated
¼ tsp chilli powder,
   (optional)

1 Combine both flours and spices in a bowl. Season with salt and pepper and make a well in the centre. Add 2 tbs oil with 330ml (1⅓ cups) cold water and whisk to a smooth batter. Set aside for 20 minutes.

2 To make mint raita, combine yoghurt, mint, coriander, ginger and chilli powder, if using, in a bowl. Season with salt and pepper, and stir to combine. Transfer to a shallow bowl.

3 Preheat oven to 100C. Line an oven tray with several layers of paper towel. Place 4cm oil in a heavy-based saucepan and heat over medium heat to 180C. (To check if oil is sufficiently hot, add a 1.5cm cube of bread to pan – if it turns golden in 35 seconds, the oil is ready.) Dip vegetable pieces in batter and allow excess batter to drip off. Using tongs and working in batches, place vegetable pieces in oil and fry for 2 minutes, turning halfway, or until golden and crisp. Using a slotted spoon, transfer vegetables to paper towel. Keep warm in oven while cooking remaining vegetables. Serve bhaji with mint raita.

*See Cooking Notes, p 92

CHEF'S TIP Ask an adult to help you deep-fry the vegetables, as you need to take good care with the hot oil (see Mexican Cooking Notes, p 190). SHOPPING LIST Tomato kasundi is a traditional spicy Indian relish. It is available from delis.

chicken with tomatoes and curry leaves

Serves: 4
Preparation: 15 mins
Cooking: 45 mins

60ml (¼ cup) vegetable oil
2 large onions, chopped
5 brown cardamom pods*
1 cinnamon quill
2 tsp ginger, finely grated
2 cloves garlic, crushed
1½ tsp ground coriander
1 tsp dried chilli flakes
½ tsp ground cumin
½ tsp ground turmeric*
1kg chicken thigh fillets,
    trimmed of excess fat,
    cut into quarters
500g ripe tomatoes,
    finely chopped
1 tsp tamarind purée*
45 fresh curry leaves*
4 paratha bread*, warmed,
    to serve

1 Heat oil in a deep, heavy-based frying pan over medium heat. Add onions and cook, stirring frequently, for 20 minutes or until golden and very soft. Add cardamom, cinnamon, ginger and garlic, and cook, stirring, for 1 minute. Add remaining spices and cook, stirring, for 30 seconds or until fragrant.

2 Add chicken to pan and cook, turning occasionally, for 5 minutes or until browned. Stir in tomatoes and tamarind purée and bring to a simmer. Reduce heat to low–medium, cover pan with a lid and cook for 10 minutes. Remove lid and cook for a further 5 minutes or until chicken is just cooked and sauce has thickened slightly.

3 Stir in curry leaves, cover and cook for a further 3 minutes. Serve with warmed paratha bread.

*See Cooking Notes, p 92

DID YOU KNOW?
The two fats commonly used in Indian cooking are clarified butter (known as ghee) and vegetable oils. The type of oil favoured depends on the region. In modern Indian cooking, corn and sunflower oils are popular for their more subtle flavour, but peanut, mustard and coconut oils are also sometimes used.

tikka lamb cutlets with coriander raita

Serves: 4
Preparation: 20 mins
+ 6 hrs marinating time
Cooking: 25 mins

140g (½ cup) Greek-style
  yoghurt
1 tbs white vinegar
3 tsp finely grated ginger
4 cloves garlic, crushed
1½ tsp ground coriander
1 tsp ground cumin
1 tsp sweet paprika
½ tsp chilli powder
  (see Chef's Tips)
¼ tsp ground cinnamon
¼ tsp ground cardamom*
12 lamb cutlets, trimmed
  of excess fat
Pappadums*, lime wedges,
  and coriander leaves,
  to serve

Coriander raita
1 small Lebanese cucumber
½ cup chopped coriander
280g (1 cup) Greek-style
  yoghurt
½ tsp ground cumin

1 Combine yoghurt, vinegar, ginger, garlic and spices in a bowl. Season with salt and pepper, and stir to combine. Add lamb and toss to combine. Cover with plastic wrap and marinate in the fridge for 6 hours or overnight (see Chef's Tips).

2 To make raita, peel cucumber and cut in half lengthwise. Using a teaspoon, scoop out seeds and discard, then chop the flesh finely. Place cucumber with remaining ingredients in a bowl. Season with salt and pepper and stir to combine.

3 Heat a chargrill pan or heavy-based frying pan over medium heat. Spray with a little oil and cook lamb, in 3 batches, for 4 minutes each side for medium–rare. Serve with coriander raita, pappadums and lime wedges, scattered with coriander leaves.

*See Cooking Notes, p 92

CHEF'S TIPS
• This is a mild dish, so double the quantity of chilli powder if you like a spicier flavour.
• The lamb can be marinated for as little as 30 minutes; however, the longer it is marinated, the better the flavour will be. Marinating it for longer also helps tenderise the meat.

creamy spiced prawns
with basmati pilau

Serves: 4
Preparation: 15 mins
+ 20 mins soaking time
Cooking: 35 mins

1½ tbs vegetable oil
1 large clove garlic, crushed
2 tsp finely grated ginger
2 tsp garam masala*
½ tsp sweet paprika
¼ tsp ground black pepper
¼ tsp ground turmeric*
¼ tsp chilli powder
900g green king prawns,
    peeled, cleaned, leaving
    tails intact (see Australian
    Cooking Notes, p 6)
1 onion, finely chopped
270ml can coconut milk
2 tsp tamarind purée*
½ cup chopped coriander
    leaves and stems, plus
    extra whole leaves,
    to serve

Basmati pilau
250g (1¼ cups)
    basmati rice
1 tbs vegetable oil
5 green cardamom pods*,
    lightly crushed
1 cinnamon quill
3 cloves
2 tsp finely grated ginger
1 clove garlic, crushed

1 To make basmati pilau, place rice in a sieve and rinse under cold running water until water runs clear. Transfer rice to a bowl, add 625ml (2½ cups) cold water and soak for 20 minutes. Drain through a sieve over a jug and reserve water.

2 Heat oil in a heavy-based saucepan over medium heat. Add cardamom, cinnamon and cloves. Cook for 30 seconds or until fragrant. Stir in ginger and garlic, and cook, stirring, for 30 seconds. Add reserved water and season with salt. Bring to the boil. Stir in rice and return to the boil. Reduce heat to low and cook, partially covered, for 10 minutes or until most of the water is absorbed and steam holes (indentations) appear in the top of the rice. Cover pan with a lid and reduce heat to very low, then steam for a further 10 minutes. Remove from heat and leave covered for a further 5 minutes before lifting the lid and fluffing rice with a fork.

3 Meanwhile, to make creamy spiced prawns, combine 2 tsp oil with garlic, ginger and spices in a bowl. Add prawns and toss to combine. Cover and set aside for 10 minutes.

4 Heat remaining 1 tbs oil in a heavy-based frying pan over medium heat. Add onion and cook, stirring, for 5 minutes or until softened. Add prawn mixture and cook, stirring occasionally, for 2 minutes. Add coconut milk and tamarind purée and bring to a simmer. Cook for 3 minutes or until prawns change colour and are cooked through, then stir in chopped coriander leaves and stems. Scatter with extra coriander leaves and serve with basmati pilau.

*See Cooking Notes, p 92

indian grilled fish with carrot and cashew pachadi

Serves: 4

Preparation: 15 mins

+ 20 mins marinating time

Cooking: 12 mins

3 tsp tamarind purée*

1 tbs lemon juice

2 cloves garlic, crushed

1 tsp finely grated ginger

1 tsp garam masala*

1 tsp ground coriander

½ tsp ground cumin

¼ tsp ground turmeric*

¼ tsp chilli powder

4 x 200g blue-eye trevalla
   fillets, skinned (see
   Shopping List)

Lime cheeks, to serve

Carrot and
cashew pachadi

1 tbs vegetable oil

1 tsp black mustard seeds*

16 fresh curry leaves*

2 large carrots,
   peeled, grated

280g (1 cup)
   Greek-style yoghurt

40g (¼ cup) roasted
   unsalted cashews,
   roughly chopped

2 tbs chopped coriander

1 Combine tamarind purée, lemon juice, garlic, ginger and spices in a bowl. Season with salt and pepper. Spread mixture all over fish. Place fish in a dish and marinate for 20 minutes.

2 To make carrot and cashew pachadi, heat oil in a saucepan over medium heat, add mustard seeds and cook, stirring, for 30 seconds or until they begin to pop. Add curry leaves, stir briefly, then add carrots and ½ tsp salt and cook, stirring regularly, for 3 minutes or until carrots are tender. Cool.

3 Combine yoghurt, cashews and coriander in a bowl, then add cooled carrot mixture and stir to combine. Season with salt and pepper.

4 Preheat a chargrill or heavy-based saucepan over medium–high heat. Cook fish for 4 minutes each side or until just cooked through (depending on thickness of fish). Serve fish with carrot and cashew pachadi and lime cheeks.

*See Cooking Notes, p 92

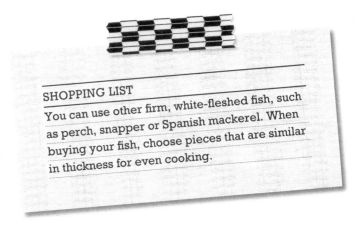

SHOPPING LIST
You can use other firm, white-fleshed fish, such as perch, snapper or Spanish mackerel. When buying your fish, choose pieces that are similar in thickness for even cooking.

beef madras curry

Serves: 4
Preparation: 20 mins
Cooking: 1 hr 55 mins

60ml (¼ cup) vegetable oil
2 large onions, chopped
800g beef chuck or blade
   steak, trimmed of excess
   fat, cut into 3cm pieces
3 cloves garlic, crushed
1 tbs finely chopped ginger
5 green cardamom pods,
   lightly crushed (see
   Cooking Notes, p 92)
1 cinnamon quill
3 tbs Madras curry paste
   (see Shopping List)
400ml can coconut milk
1 long green chilli,
   halved lengthwise
Steamed basmati rice,
   to serve

1 Heat oil in a heavy-based frying pan over medium heat. Add onions and cook, stirring frequently, for 20 minutes or until golden and very soft. Add beef and cook, stirring, for 3 minutes or until browned.

2 Add garlic, ginger and spices, and cook, stirring, for 1 minute. Add curry paste and cook, stirring, for 1 minute.

3 Stir in coconut milk and 180ml (¾ cup) water and chilli. Bring to a simmer. Reduce heat to low, cover pan with a lid and cook, stirring occasionally for 1½ hours or until beef is very tender. Serve with steamed rice.

SHOPPING LIST Madras curry paste is available at selected supermarkets. TIME SAVER Curry can be made up to 2 days ahead. Store in an airtight container in the refrigerator, or freeze for up to 2 months. Reheat in a saucepan until bubbling.

ENGLAND

Liverpool • Manchester

• Birmingham

Oxford •
London

ENGLA

The first pies are said to date back to 9500 BC!

To drive a London cab, you need to pass a test called 'the knowledge'. To eat sticky date pud, you just need a spoon!

ND

MACARONI CHEESE

*

BACON AND EGG PIE

*

SAGE-ROASTED PORK
LOIN WITH ROASTED
POTATOES AND APPLES

*

COTTAGE PIE

*

SELF-SAUCING
STICKY DATE PUDDING

*

VICTORIA SPONGE CAKE
WITH JAM AND CREAM

ENGLAND COOKING NOTES

TO TEST IF A CAKE IS DONE Using oven gloves, remove the cake from the oven and gently insert a skewer through the centre of the cake to the bottom of the pan. Slowly pull out the skewer: if the skewer is clean, the cake is done; if the skewer has uncooked batter on it, continue cooking the cake.

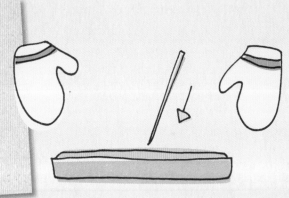

Potato varieties

Waxy High in moisture but low in starch, they hold their shape when boiled. They can be added to stews and are good in salads. Varieties include: purple congo (1), kipfler (6), nicola and pink fir apple.

Floury Low in moisture and sugar but high in starch. Best for mashing, frying and roasting. Varieties include: coliban (baby colibans are known as chats) and king edwards.

All-rounders Suit baking, roasting, mashing and steaming. Varieties include: red delight (2), golden delight (3), desiree (4), cream delight (5) and sebago (baby sebagos are also sold as chats).

ON A ROLL

Tying large joints of meat for roasting gives them a more compact shape, so they cook more evenly. To tie a pork loin, you'll need kitchen string, available from supermarkets. Roll up pork with your hands, then, starting 3cm in from one end, tie a length of string tightly around meat and knot it. Repeat at the other end of the meat, then work in towards the centre to form a compact shape.

PERFECT PASTRY Make sure your butter is chilled and try to work quickly so the pastry doesn't soften too much. If your pastry gets too soft after rolling, place it on a tray and refrigerate for 10 minutes to firm. And if your pastry cracks when you're lining your tin, don't worry – simply patch it up with offcuts!

HP is said to stand for Houses of Parliament, where it was served.

Season to taste

Worcestershire Sauce Invented in the city of Worcester by Mr Lea and Mr Perrins in the 1830s. Its spicy flavour is derived from chilli, tamarind, molasses, garlic, cloves and more!
Keen's Mustard Keen's was founded more than 100 years ago in Durham. It comes in powder or paste form.
HP Sauce Since the early 1900s, this classic 'brown sauce' has been the condiment of choice for a great British fry-up! Its 'secret recipe' includes dates, apple juice, garlic and spices.

macaroni cheese

Serves: 6
Preparation: 20 mins
Cooking: 1 hr

225g (1¼ cups)
    macaroni pasta
4 bacon rashers, rind
    removed, chopped
2 tbs fresh breadcrumbs
    (see Italian Cooking
    Notes, p 38)
Green salad, to serve

Cheese sauce
40g butter
1 onion, finely chopped
2 tbs plain flour
500ml (2 cups) milk
180g (1½ cups) grated
    tasty cheddar
50g (⅔ cup) grated
    parmesan
Pinch mustard powder
    (see Cooking Notes,
    p 108)

1 Preheat oven to 200C. Cook pasta in a large saucepan of boiling salted water according to packet instructions or until al dente (see Italian Cooking Notes, p 38). Drain in a colander and toss with a little olive oil and transfer to a bowl.

2 Heat a non-stick frying pan over medium heat and cook bacon, stirring occasionally, until crisp. Add bacon and any pan drippings to the pasta and toss to combine.

3 To make the cheese sauce, melt butter in a saucepan over low heat, add onion and cook for 5 minutes or until softened. Add flour and stir continuously for 1 minute or until mixture is bubbling. Remove from heat and stir in milk, 2 tbs at a time (the flour mixture will absorb the milk and clump together). Continue adding milk, stirring after each addition until combined (after the third addition, it should start to become smooth). Stir in remaining milk, return to a low–medium heat and cook, stirring continuously, until mixture comes to the boil and thickens.

4 Add ¾ cup cheddar, the parmesan and mustard powder, and stir to combine. Season with salt and pepper. Pour sauce over pasta mixture and stir to combine. Spoon mixture into a 1.5-litre (6-cup) ovenproof dish, smooth top and scatter over breadcrumbs and remaining cheddar.

5 Bake for 40 minutes or until browned on top and bubbling. Stand for 5 minutes before serving with salad.

MIX & MATCH Stir in 165g (1 cup) fresh corn kernels to macaroni mixture before cooking, or slice 2 tomatoes and place on top of macaroni, before adding parmesan and breadcrumbs.

bacon and egg pie

Serves: 6

Preparation: 30 mins
+ 30 mins refrigeration time

Cooking: 30 mins

6 rashers bacon,
  rind removed
6 spring onions, chopped
8 eggs
1 egg, lightly beaten with
  1 tbs water, for egg wash
Tomato chutney, to serve

Pastry
250g (1²⁄₃ cups) plain flour
150g cold unsalted butter,
  chopped
1 egg, lightly beaten

CHEF'S TIP Placing the pie on a preheated oven tray will help the base of the pastry to cook through.
TIME SAVER Instead of making your own pastry for the bacon and egg pie, use 2 sheets of frozen shortcrust pastry for the base and 2 sheets of frozen puff pastry for the top.

1 To make pastry, sift flour into a bowl and add butter. Using fingertips, rub in butter until mixture resembles breadcrumbs. Add egg and 2 tbs iced water and, using a butter knife, stir to combine until mixture just comes together. Transfer dough to a lightly floured work surface and knead until smooth. Divide into two discs, one slightly larger than the other, wrap in plastic wrap and refrigerate for 30 minutes.

2 Place an oven tray in oven (see Chef's Tip) and preheat oven to 190C. Roll larger pastry disc between two sheets of baking paper until large enough to line a 23cm pie pan. Drape pastry over the rolling pin, lift pastry into pan, then trim the edge.

3 Place 3 bacon rashers over pastry base and sprinkle over half the spring onions. Break 4 eggs, one at a time, into a cup, then place on bacon. Pierce each yolk with a knife and season with pepper. Repeat with remaining bacon, spring onions and eggs. Season and brush pastry edge with egg wash.

4 Roll out remaining pastry disc until large enough to cover the pie, then, using the rolling pin to lift the pastry, place it over filling, pressing pastry edges to seal. Trim excess pastry, then crimp edges. Brush top with egg wash.

5 Place pie on preheated oven tray and bake for 30 minutes or until golden and eggs are cooked. Cool pie for 10 minutes before serving with tomato chutney.

sage-roasted pork loin with roasted potatoes and apples

Serves: 6

Preparation: 15 mins
+ 4 hrs refrigeration time

Cooking: 2 hrs 40 mins

1.5kg boned, untied loin
  of pork, scored
2 tsp sage leaves,
  thinly sliced
60ml (¼ cup) olive oil
1 large red onion, cut into
  thick rounds
1kg sebago or coliban
  potatoes (see Cooking
  Notes, p 108), peeled,
  cut into 3cm pieces
3 pink lady apples, cored,
  cut into 3cm pieces
2 tsp brown sugar
10g butter, chopped

Gravy
2 tbs cornflour
250ml (1 cup) apple juice
125ml (½ cup) vegetable
  or chicken stock

1 Preheat oven to 220C. Place pork, skin-side up, on a clean work surface and rub skin with 1 tsp salt. Transfer pork onto a wire rack in a roasting pan and refrigerate for 4 hours or overnight to dry out skin (this will help make the crackling crisp when cooked).

2 Place pork, skin-side down, on a clean work surface, season with pepper and scatter with sage. Drizzle with 1 tbs oil and rub pepper and sage into the pork. Roll up the pork and tie with kitchen string (see Cooking Notes, p 108).

3 Scatter onion in a roasting pan and place pork, skin-side up, on top. Roast for 25 minutes. Reduce heat to 200C and cook for a further 1 hour. Toss potatoes with 1 tbs oil and season with salt. Place potatoes around pork in pan, return to oven and cook for a further 1 hour, turning potatoes halfway. To check if pork is cooked, pierce with a sharp knife; if juices run clear, pork is cooked. Cover loosely with foil and rest for 20 minutes.

4 Meanwhile, place apples in a roasting pan, toss with remaining oil and season. Bake for 10 minutes, then sprinkle with sugar and dot with butter. Turn apples and bake for a further 15 minutes or until lightly caramelised and softened.

5 To make gravy, drain off all but 2 tbs fat from pork roasting pan, while leaving meat juices in pan. Add cornflour to pan, stirring to combine, then cook over low heat, stirring continuously, for 2 minutes. Add apple juice and stock, and stir, scraping all the bits from the base of the pan. Bring to the boil and simmer for 2 minutes. Strain gravy through a sieve into a jug.

6 Transfer pork to a chopping board, remove string, then slice thickly. Serve with roasted potatoes, apples and gravy.

cottage pie

Serves: 4–6
Preparation: 30 mins
Cooking: 1 hr 10 mins

2 tbs olive oil
1 onion, chopped
1 clove garlic, crushed
1 celery stalk, chopped
1 carrot, chopped
750g minced beef
70g (¼ cup) tomato paste
310ml (1¼ cups) beef stock
1 tbs Worcestershire sauce*
35g (¼ cup) cornflour
2 tbs chopped flat-leaf
    parsley
Steamed broccoli and
    beans, to serve

Potato topping
1kg coliban or king edward
    potatoes*, peeled,
    chopped
60g butter, chopped
80ml (⅓ cup) milk

1 Heat oil in a large, heavy-based saucepan over low heat. Add onion, garlic, celery and carrot, and cook, stirring occasionally, for 10 minutes or until vegetables are softened. Increase heat to medium, add mince and cook, stirring, for 5 minutes or until browned, breaking up the mince with a wooden spoon.

2 Add tomato paste, stock and Worcestershire sauce, stir to combine, then bring to the boil. Reduce heat to low–medium and simmer for 5 minutes. Combine cornflour with 60ml (¼ cup) water and stir to form a paste. Add to pan and cook, stirring occasionally, for 5 minutes or until mixture has thickened. Season with salt and pepper. Stir in parsley, then transfer mixture to a 2-litre (8-cup) ovenproof dish.

3 Preheat oven to 200C. To make potato topping, place potatoes in a large saucepan, cover with cold water and add a pinch of salt. Bring to the boil and cook for 15 minutes or until potatoes are tender. Drain well, return to saucepan and mash with a potato masher until smooth. Add 40g chopped butter and milk, then season. Spoon mashed potato over filling, level, then, using a fork, roughen the top. Dot with remaining 20g butter and bake for 30 minutes or until top is golden. Serve cottage pie with steamed broccoli and beans.

*See Cooking Notes, p 108

MIX & MATCH To make individual pies, use 6 x 250ml (1-cup) ramekins. Use chopped leftover roast beef instead of mince. For shepherd's pie, use minced lamb or chopped leftover roast lamb.

self-saucing sticky date pudding

Serves: 6
Preparation: 20 mins
Cooking: 25 mins

185g (1¼ cups)
 self-raising flour
165g (¾ cup, firmly packed)
 brown sugar
90g (⅔ cup) pitted dried
 dates, chopped
180ml (¾ cup) milk
30g butter, melted
Pouring cream, to serve

Caramel sauce
165g (¾ cup, firmly packed)
 brown sugar
60g butter, chopped

1 Preheat oven to 180C. Lightly grease 6 x 250ml (1-cup) ramekins and place on an oven tray. Combine flour and sugar in a bowl, add dates and stir to combine. Add milk and melted butter, and stir to form a sticky batter. Spoon batter into prepared ramekins and smooth tops.

2 To make caramel sauce, combine sugar, butter and 500ml (2 cups) water in a saucepan and stir over medium heat until sugar is dissolved and butter is melted. Bring to the boil, then remove from heat. Pour sauce over the back of a wooden spoon onto batter in ramekins (see Chef's Tips).

3 Transfer the oven tray to the oven and bake puddings for 20 minutes or until firm to the touch. Stand for 5 minutes, then serve with pouring cream.

CHEF'S TIPS
• Using the back of a spoon helps to pour the caramel slowly and evenly.
• Make a large pudding by buttering a 2-litre (8-cup) ovenproof dish. Spoon batter into dish and pour over sauce. Bake at 180C for 45 minutes or until firm to the touch.

victoria sponge cake with jam and cream

Serves: 6
Preparation: 20 mins
Cooking: 30 mins

225g unsalted butter,
  softened
220g (1 cup) caster sugar
4 eggs
225g (1½ cups) self-raising
  flour
2 tsp baking powder
1 tsp vanilla extract
Icing sugar, to dust

Filling
110g (⅓ cup) strawberry
  or raspberry jam
250ml (1 cup) thickened
  cream, whipped until thick

1 To make sponge, preheat oven to 180C. Lightly grease 6 x 9cm (base measurement) individual springform pans or 2 x 20cm sandwich cake pans and line with baking paper. Using an electric mixer, beat butter, sugar, eggs, flour, baking powder and vanilla extract on low speed until well combined. Increase speed to high and beat for 3 minutes or until mixture is smooth and pale.

2 Divide mixture among prepared pans, then, using a spatula, smooth the tops. Bake for 30 minutes (for both cake sizes) or until a skewer inserted in the centre comes out clean (see Cooking Notes, p 108). Cool cakes in pans for 5 minutes, then turn out each cake onto a wire rack and remove baking paper. Cool cakes completely before decorating.

3 To assemble small cakes, using a serrated knife, cut cakes in half horizontally. Spread bottom half with jam, leaving a 1cm border, then spread with cream. Sandwich with tops and dust with icing sugar to serve. For a large cake, place 1 x 20cm cake on a platter and spread over jam, then cream, as for small cakes. Top with second cake, then dust top with icing sugar to serve.

CHEF'S TIPS
• Fill the cake with fresh raspberries and sliced strawberries when in season, together with the jam and the whipped cream.
• This sponge freezes well and can be used for cassata cake recipe, page 52.

FRANCE

OEUFS FRAIS

MERCI BEAUCOUP

The Eiffel Tower is France's most iconic structure (built in 1889).

MUSSELS IN WHITE WINE
*
PAN BAGNAT WITH TUNA,
OLIVES AND ROASTED TOMATOES
*
LEEK AND GRUYERE QUICHE
WITH GREEN SALAD
*
SIRLOIN STEAKS WITH ASPARAGUS
AND CHIVE HOLLANDAISE
*
ROAST TARRAGON CHICKEN WITH
CREAMY PARIS MASH
*
CREPES WITH ORANGE SAUCE
*
CHOCOLATE SOUFFLE WITH
RASPBERRY COULIS

FRANCE COOKING NOTES

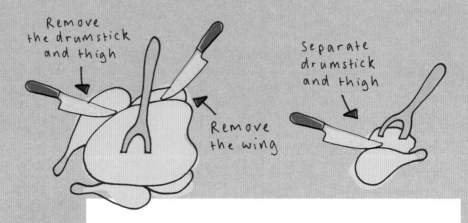

Remove
the drumstick
and thigh

Remove
the wing

Separate
drumstick
and thigh

CHERVIL

This herb has a mild aniseed
flavour and is a member of
the parsley family, for which it
can be substituted. The classic
French herb mix *fines herbes*
is made from chervil, chives,
parsley and tarragon.

To carve a chicken

Get an adult to help you. Place chicken on a non-slip board,
breast side up. Remove the string. Using a carving fork to
steady the chicken, insert a large knife between the body and
leg and remove the drumstick and thigh in one piece. Separate
the drumstick and thigh by cutting through the joint. Remove
the wing on the same side by cutting through the joint. Slice the
breast into 1cm-thick slices. Repeat this on the other side.

VERJUICE is unripe grape juice
that's used in similar ways to
lemon juice or vinegar, but is less
acidic. Depending on the recipe,
substitute with dry white wine,
white wine vinegar or lemon juice.
It's available from supermarkets
and delis.

Crêpe pan

While you can cook crêpes in any small, non-stick frying pan, using one of these special crêpe pans will make the task a lot easier, especially if you're keen to try your hand at flipping them over! The shallow rim will help you to flip like a professional, while also giving you a nice, even finish to the edge of each crêpe.

QUICHE LORRAINE The quiche recipe on page 130 is an adaptation of this classic dish from Lorraine in north-east France, which was once part of Germany. The word 'quiche' comes from the German word *küchen* (cake). It was originally made with a bread base and is traditionally filled with eggs, cream and smoked bacon.

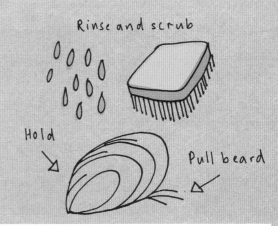

Rinse and scrub

Hold

Pull beard

TARRAGON

Two types of tarragon are sold in Australia: French and Russian. The French variety is superior, with a stronger aniseed fragrance and flavour. Look for long, narrow, smooth-edged spear-like leaves. Russian tarragon has less shiny, more jagged, serrated leaves.

Cleaning and bearding mussels

Rinse mussels under cold running water. Using a clean scourer or brush, scrub shells to remove any barnacles and sand. To remove the furry beard, hold mussel firmly in one hand while pulling the beard away with the other. Discard any mussels that don't close when tapped sharply. Ready-cleaned mussels are available in packs from selected fishmongers and supermarkets.

mussels in white wine

Serves: 4
Preparation: 15 mins
Cooking: 25 mins

25g butter
1 onion, finely chopped
2 cloves garlic, crushed
1 tbs chopped thyme leaves
180ml (¾ cup) verjuice*
60ml (¼ cup) dry
    white wine
2kg black mussels,
    scrubbed, bearded*
125ml (½ cup)
    pouring cream
2 tbs chopped flat-leaf
    parsley
Crusty bread, to serve

1 Melt butter in a saucepan over medium heat. Add onion and cook, stirring occasionally, for 10 minutes or until softened. Add garlic and thyme, and cook, stirring, for 1 minute or until fragrant. Add verjuice and wine, bring to the boil, then simmer for 1 minute.

2 Turn heat to high and add mussels. Cover with a tight-fitting lid and cook, shaking pan occasionally, for 4 minutes or until mussels are open. Using tongs, transfer open mussels to a large bowl. Cook remaining mussels for a further 2 minutes and transfer to bowl. Discard any unopened mussels.

3 Add cream to saucepan and simmer for 3 minutes or until slightly thickened. Stir in parsley and season with salt and pepper. Divide mussels among 4 large bowls and ladle over sauce. Serve with crusty bread.

*See Cooking Notes, p 124

MIX & MATCH For a Mediterranean version, replace the cream with a 400g can chopped tomatoes.

pan bagnat with tuna, olives and roasted tomatoes

Serves: 4–6

Preparation: 20 mins
+ cooling time
+ overnight refrigeration

Cooking: 1½ hrs

4 large ripe roma tomatoes,
  halved lengthwise
1 tbs olive oil
450g small pagnotta or
  other small woodfired
  crusty loaf
1 clove garlic,
  peeled, halved
2 tsp red wine vinegar
2 tbs extra virgin olive oil
425g can tuna in oil,
  drained
16 large basil leaves
40g (¼ cup) sliced, pitted
  kalamata olives
110g (½ cup) marinated
  artichokes, drained,
  halved if large

1 Preheat oven to 150C. Place tomatoes, cut-side up, on an oven tray lined with baking paper, drizzle with olive oil and season with salt and pepper. Roast for 1½ hours or until starting to wrinkle. Turn off oven and leave tomatoes in oven until cool. Transfer to an airtight container and refrigerate until needed.

2 Carefully slice bread in half horizontally, keeping both sides as even as possible. Using your fingers or a small knife, remove most of the bread in middle of each half, leaving a 2cm shell. Rub bread shell with cut sides of garlic clove. Combine vinegar and extra virgin olive oil in a bowl and brush inside both sides of bread with oil mixture. Spoon tuna evenly into bottom half of shell, top with basil leaves, olives, tomatoes and artichokes. Replace top half of bread and wrap loaf tightly in plastic wrap, then foil. Place bread on a tray, then place a chopping board on top. Place 4 food cans or other weights on top of the board (to compress the filling) and refrigerate overnight. Cut bread into wedges to serve.

MIX & MATCH 'Pan bagnat' loosely translates as 'bathed bread'. The filling can be varied according to your taste. Try adding sliced hard-boiled egg, rocket, cucumber or anchovies.

CHEF'S TIP Don't throw away bread pieces removed from the shell. Turn them into croûtons. Toss bread pieces in olive oil and spread on an oven tray. Bake at 200C for 10 minutes or until golden and crisp. Use them scattered over soups or tossed through salads.

leek and gruyère quiche with green salad

Serves: 4–6
Preparation: 40 mins
+ 1 hr chilling time
+ 25 mins cooling time
Cooking: 55 mins

2 tbs olive oil
2 large leeks, white part
   only, halved lengthwise,
   thinly sliced
2 cloves garlic, crushed
1 tbs chopped chervil*
   or flat-leaf parsley
3 eggs, lightly beaten
180ml (¾ cup)
   pouring cream
45g (½ cup) grated gruyère

Pastry
265g (1¾ cups) plain flour
150g cold butter, chopped

Green salad
1 tbs red wine vinegar
2 tbs extra virgin olive oil
1 tbs walnut oil (or extra
   virgin olive oil)
½ tsp Dijon mustard
½ tsp caster sugar
100g mixed salad leaves
2 tbs walnuts, roughly
   chopped

1 To make pastry, process flour and butter in a food processor until mixture resembles breadcrumbs. Add 2½ tbs cold water and pulse until mixture just comes together. Gently knead dough on a lightly floured work surface until smooth. Form into a disc and wrap in plastic wrap. Refrigerate for 30 minutes.

2 Roll out pastry between 2 sheets of baking paper until large enough to line a 24cm x 5cm-deep round tart pan with removable base. Press pastry into pan and trim edge with a knife. Cover with plastic wrap and refrigerate for 30 minutes.

3 Preheat oven to 200C. Remove plastic wrap. Line pastry with baking paper and fill with dried beans or rice (see Chef's Tip). Place tart on an oven tray and bake for 15 minutes. Remove paper and beans, and bake for a further 15 minutes or until light golden. Cool for 15 minutes. Reduce oven temperature to 180C.

4 Meanwhile, heat oil in a saucepan and cook leeks and garlic, stirring occasionally, over low–medium heat, for 10 minutes or until very soft. Stand for 5 minutes to cool slightly. Spread leek mixture over base of tart shell. Scatter with chervil. Whisk eggs and cream in a small jug and season with salt and pepper. Pour egg mixture over leek mixture and scatter with gruyère. Bake for 25 minutes or until just set. Cool tart for 5 minutes before serving.

5 To make green salad, combine vinegar, oils, mustard and caster sugar in a screw-top jar. Shake until well combined. Combine salad leaves and walnuts in a bowl, drizzle with dressing and toss gently. Serve slices of quiche with green salad.

*See Cooking Notes, p 124

CHEF'S TIP Cooking a tart case in this way is called 'blind baking' and gives a nice crisp finish to the pastry.

sirloin steaks with asparagus and chive hollandaise

Serves: 4

Preparation: 10 mins

+ 5 mins resting time

Cooking: 10 mins

4 x 200g sirloin steaks

Olive oil, to brush

2 bunches asparagus

Oven-baked frozen French
  fries, to serve

Chive hollandaise

125g butter, chopped

2 egg yolks

1 tbs white wine vinegar

¼ tsp coarse ground
  black pepper

2 tsp chopped chives

1 Preheat a barbecue or chargrill pan to high. Brush both sides of steaks with oil. Season with salt and pepper. Barbecue or chargrill steaks for 4 minutes each side, depending on thickness, for medium–rare. Transfer steaks to a plate, cover with foil and rest for 5 minutes (see Chef's Tips).

2 Meanwhile, to make chive hollandaise, melt butter in a small saucepan over low heat, then transfer to a heatproof jug. Place egg yolks, vinegar and pepper in a food processor. Process for 20 seconds or until well combined. With motor running, gradually add butter through a funnel, pouring in a thin stream. Process until thick. Transfer hollandaise to a bowl, season and stir in chives.

3 Cook asparagus in a saucepan of boiling water for 2 minutes or until just tender. Drain. Divide steaks and asparagus among plates, drizzle with chive hollandaise and serve with French fries.

CHEF'S TIPS
• Resting the steaks allows the juices to 'settle' into the meat resulting in a tender, juicy steak.
• Hollandaise sauce is best made close to serving. Set aside in a warm place if necessary. Don't let it get too hot or too cold and discard any leftover sauce.
• To chop chives, use scissors to cut them into small lengths.

roast tarragon chicken with creamy paris mash

Serves: 4–6

Preparation: 30 mins
+ 20 mins resting time

Cooking: 1 hr 45 mins

50g butter, softened

1 clove garlic, crushed

1 tsp finely grated
   lemon zest

1 tbs chopped tarragon*
   plus 2 sprigs
   tarragon, extra

1.7kg free-range chicken

½ lemon

1 tbs olive oil

180ml (¾ cup)
   chicken stock

60ml (¼ cup) verjuice*
   (or dry white wine)

Steamed green vegetables,
   to serve

Paris mash

1kg desiree potatoes,
   peeled, chopped

150ml pouring cream

60g butter, chopped

1 Preheat oven to 200C. Combine butter, garlic, lemon zest and chopped tarragon in a bowl. Season with salt and pepper. Using your fingertips, gently push your fingers between the skin and the breast of the chicken, easing skin away from flesh, taking care not to tear the skin. Spread half of the butter mixture evenly over flesh. Place extra tarragon sprigs and lemon inside cavity of the chicken. Tie legs together with kitchen string. Place chicken on a rack in a roasting pan. Rub chicken with olive oil and dot remaining butter mixture over top of chicken. Season.

2 Roast chicken for 1 hour. Combine stock and verjuice and pour over chicken. Roast for a further 45 minutes (cover with foil if chicken is over-browning) or until golden and the juices run clear when the thickest part of the thigh is pierced. Cover chicken with foil and rest in a warm place for 20 minutes.

3 Meanwhile, to make Paris mash, place potatoes in a saucepan and cover with cold water. Bring to the boil and cook for 20 minutes or until very tender. Drain well in a colander. Dry the same pan, then return potatoes to pan and cook over low heat for 1 minute or until potatoes are very dry. Using a mouli or masher, purée potatoes. Transfer to a clean saucepan. Heat cream and butter in a small saucepan over low heat until butter is melted and cream is hot. Gradually pour cream mixture into potato, beating well with a wooden spoon until smooth. Season with salt and pepper.

4 Ask an adult to help you carve the chicken (see Cooking Notes, p 124). Drizzle chicken with pan juices, then serve with Paris mash and steamed green vegetables.

*See Cooking Notes, p 124

crêpes with orange sauce

Serves: 4

Preparation: 15 mins
+ 30 mins resting time

Cooking: 35 mins

150g (1 cup) plain flour
3 eggs, lightly beaten
500ml (2 cups) milk
40g melted ghee
    (clarified butter)
2 oranges, peeled, white
    pith removed, sliced
    widthwise
Vanilla ice-cream, to serve

Orange sauce
250ml (1 cup) freshly
    squeezed orange juice
220g (1 cup) caster sugar
50g butter, chopped

MIX & MATCH To make
a rich chocolate sauce,
heat 200ml cream in
a saucepan until just
boiling. Remove pan
from heat and add 150g
finely chopped dark
chocolate (70% cocoa
solids). Set aside for
a few minutes to melt
chocolate, then stir
until smooth. Sauce will
thicken on cooling.

1 To make orange sauce, combine juice and sugar in a saucepan over medium heat. Stir until sugar has dissolved, then bring to the boil and simmer for 10 minutes or until reduced by one-quarter. Remove from heat, then gradually add butter, 1 piece at a time, whisking until it has melted and combined before adding the next. Whisk until all the butter is incorporated, then set aside and keep warm.

2 To make crêpes, sift flour into a bowl. Combine eggs and milk in a jug. Slowly add egg mixture to flour, whisking well, until mixture is smooth. Set aside for 30 minutes to rest batter.

3 Heat a 22cm non-stick crêpe pan or non-stick frying pan over medium heat. Brush with a little ghee. Pour 60ml (¼ cup) crêpe batter into pan, tilting pan and swirling batter to cover base of the pan with a thin coating. Cook for 1 minute or until lightly browned underneath. Using a spatula, carefully turn crêpe over and cook for a further minute or until lightly browned. Slide crêpe onto a plate and cover with a tea towel to keep warm. Repeat with remaining mixture to make 12 crêpes.

4 Fold crêpes into quarters, then serve with orange slices, orange sauce and vanilla ice-cream.

chocolate soufflé with raspberry coulis

Serves: 4
Preparation: 35 mins
Cooking: 15 mins

20g unsalted butter,
    softened
2 tbs white sugar
100g dark chocolate
    (70% cocoa solids),
    chopped
25g unsalted butter
2 egg yolks, lightly beaten
4 egg whites, at room
    temperature
1½ tbs caster sugar
Icing sugar, to dust
Vanilla ice-cream, to serve

Raspberry coulis
300g pkt frozen
    raspberries, thawed
2½ tbs icing sugar

CHEF'S TIP As a soufflé starts to deflate very quickly after it's been removed from the oven, have everything ready: the guests seated at the table, the serving plates, the ice-cream scooped in side dishes and coulis poured into a serving jug. As chefs say, "A soufflé waits for no one!"

1 To make raspberry coulis, place raspberries and their juice, and icing sugar in a food processor. Process for 1 minute or until puréed. Push purée through a sieve with the back of a spoon into a bowl. Discard seeds. Cover coulis and refrigerate until needed.

2 Working from the base up the side, brush 4 x 160ml (⅔-cup) ovenproof ramekins thickly with softened butter (this will help the soufflés to rise). Pour white sugar into 1 ramekin. Rotate ramekin to coat base and sides, then pour remaining sugar into next ramekin. Repeat with remaining ramekins. Discard any leftover sugar.

3 Preheat oven to 220C. Fill a saucepan one-third full with water and bring to a gentle simmer. Place chocolate and butter in a heatproof bowl, then place bowl over saucepan and stir until melted (don't allow the bowl touch the water). Remove the bowl from the saucepan, add egg yolks and stir gently to combine.

4 Using an electric mixer, beat egg whites until soft peaks form. Gradually add caster sugar and beat until firm peaks just form. Gently fold one-third of the egg whites into chocolate mixture to loosen mixture. Then gently fold remaining egg whites into chocolate mixture. Do not over-mix – you need to keep as much air in the soufflés as possible. Divide mixture among prepared dishes. (Run your finger around the inside rim of the ramekin to stop mixture sticking to edge and help the soufflé to rise.) Place soufflés on an oven tray and cook for 10 minutes or until well risen. Dust soufflés with icing sugar, then serve immediately with raspberry coulis and vanilla ice-cream.

JAPAN

The soy sauce bottle is shaped like a fish to serve with sushi. Too cute!

The Japanese believe food should reflect nature and look as pretty as a picture.

Sapporo

JAPAN

Tokyo
Kyoto

Hiroshima

SUSHI HAND ROLLS
*
PRAWN AND VEGETABLE
TEMPURA
*
BEEF AND VEGETABLE
ROLLS
*
PORK TONKATSU WITH
SESAME COLESLAW
*
YAKITORI CHICKEN
AND VEGETABLES
*
TERIYAKI SALMON
*
GREEN BEANS WITH
SESAME MISO DRESSING

JAPAN COOKING NOTES

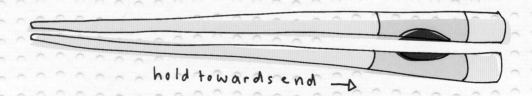

hold towards end →

JAPANESE CHOPSTICKS ETIQUETTE
• Hold chopsticks towards the end, not the middle.
• Don't spear your food, point, or wave them around.
• Don't stick them upright in rice; this is a funeral ritual.
• Don't use chopsticks to move plates or bowls.
• Use the opposite ends to pick up food from shared plates.
• After you've finished eating, place chopsticks in front of you with the tips facing towards the left.

The basics: part 1

Rice vinegar This is often made from other grains as well as rice. Available from supermarkets.
Japanese soy sauce Known as shoyu, it has a slightly sweeter flavour than other styles. Available from Asian grocers and selected supermarkets.
Mirin This sweet Japanese rice wine is available from supermarkets in different grades. For the best flavour, use Manjo mirin or other brands of hon ('true') mirin.
Sake This Japanese rice wine is available from liquor stores. Cooking sake is available from selected Asian grocers.

Japanese soy sauce

sake

rice vinegar

mirin

The basics: part 2

1 Dashi A powdered soup stock made from dried bonito tuna flakes and dried seaweed. Available from Asian grocers.

2 Nori Seaweed sheets are available from supermarkets and Asian grocers. You can buy them untoasted or toasted. To toast nori, using tongs, hold a sheet of nori 20cm above a gas flame for 30 seconds, or dry-fry in a frying pan over low heat for 20 seconds.

3 Panko breadcrumbs Available from Asian grocers and selected supermarkets. Substitute regular dried breadcrumbs.

4 Wasabi paste Available from Asian grocers and supermarkets. Fresh wasabi (Japanese horseradish) is available from selected greengrocers in winter.

5 Daikon A long white radish, available from greengrocers and Asian grocers.

MISO PASTE

Miso is a mixture of fermented soybeans and sometimes grains. There are three basic varieties: mame miso (soybeans only); mugi miso (soybeans and barley); and kome miso (soybeans and rice). Aka miso (red miso) is a salty variety of kome or mugi miso that's been fermented for a year, while shiro miso (white miso) is made with less fermentation and has a sweeter flavour. You'll find a variety of miso pastes at Asian grocers; a more limited selection (including white and red miso pastes) is available from selected supermarkets.

RICE Japanese short-grain rice is available in hundreds of varieties. Koshihikari and Sasanishiki are popular ones. In Australia, you can use SunRice sushi rice, available from supermarkets.

sushi hand rolls

Makes: 12
Preparation: 20 mins
+ 40 mins draining
and standing time
Cooking: 12 mins

3 sheets toasted nori*
1 tbs rice vinegar*
2 tsp wasabi paste*
100g smoked salmon,
    cut into 3cm-wide strips
1 Lebanese cucumber,
    halved, seeded, sliced
    lengthwise into batons
1 tbs mayonnaise
6 cooked prawns,
    peeled, cleaned
    (see Australian Cooking
    Notes, p 6)
1 avocado, stone removed,
    flesh sliced lengthwise
    (see Mexican Cooking
    Notes, p 190)
Japanese soy sauce
    (shoyu)*, to serve

Sushi rice
300g (1½ cups) sushi rice*
60ml (¼ cup) rice vinegar
1½ tbs caster sugar

1 To make sushi rice, place rice in a sieve and rinse under running cold water until water runs clear. Stand rice in sieve for 30 minutes to drain well. Meanwhile, stir vinegar, sugar and ¼ tsp salt in a bowl until sugar dissolves.

2 Place drained rice and 375ml (1½ cups) water in a saucepan and bring to the boil. Cover with a lid, reduce heat to very low and cook for 12 minutes. Stand, covered, for 10 minutes.

3 Spread rice out in a stainless-steel bowl. Using a spatula, slice through rice, breaking up any lumps. While doing this, gradually add vinegar mixture. To give rice a sheen, continue lifting and turning the rice, while with the other hand (or get an adult to help), fan rice for 5 minutes or until almost cool. Don't over-cool rice or it will harden. Cover rice with a clean, damp tea towel to prevent it drying out.

4 Cut each nori sheet into 4 equal pieces and cover with plastic wrap to prevent them drying out. Combine rice vinegar with 125ml (½ cup) water in a bowl.

5 To make sushi hand rolls, place a piece of nori, shiny-side down, diagonally across palm of your hand. Lightly dip two fingers in vinegared water, then pick up 2 tbs rice and place in centre of nori. Using your other hand, spread rice towards top corner of nori, leaving the bottom and sides uncovered. Make a groove in the middle of the rice for fillings. For the first filling, place a dab of wasabi over rice and top with a piece of salmon and 2 cucumber batons. Fold nori over filling to form a cone, wetting edge with vinegared water and pressing gently to seal. Repeat to make 5 more. Then make 6 more, this time filling with rice, a dab of mayonnaise, a prawn and 2 slices of avocado. Serve with soy sauce, wasabi paste and mayonnaise.

*See Cooking Notes, p 142

prawn and vegetable tempura

Serves: 4
Preparation: 20 mins
Cooking: 20 mins

8 green king prawns
Vegetable oil, to deep-fry
(see Mexican Cooking
Notes, p 190)
200g pumpkin, peeled, cut
into 4mm-thick slices (get
an adult to help you)
1 small head broccoli,
cut into florets
8 small button mushrooms,
stalks trimmed
1 Japanese eggplant, cut
into 3mm-thick slices
on the diagonal
12 green beans, trimmed
Plain flour, to dust

Dipping sauce
½ tsp dashi granules*
80ml (⅓ cup) mirin*
80ml (⅓ cup) light
soy sauce (see Chinese
Cooking Notes, p74)
½ cup finely grated daikon*,
squeezed dry (optional)

Tempura batter
1 egg
430ml (1¾) cups chilled
soda water
150g (1 cup) plain flour
150g (1 cup) cornflour

1 To make sauce, combine dashi granules, mirin, soy sauce and 250ml (1 cup) water in a saucepan. Bring just to the boil, then remove and keep warm. To serve, roll grated daikon (if using) into 4 small balls, then place in 4 small dipping bowls with sauce.

2 Peel prawns, leaving tails intact (see Australian Cooking Notes, p 6). Using a small, sharp knife, cut a few incisions along belly to prevent prawns curling. Pat prawns dry with paper towel.

3 To make tempura batter, place egg in a large bowl and whisk until lightly beaten, then stir in soda water. Add flours and, using a chopstick or butter knife, roughly stir ingredients until almost combined (there should still be a few lumps in the batter).

4 Preheat oven to 100C. Fill a deep-fryer or large saucepan one-third full with oil and heat over medium heat to 180C – get an adult to help you. (To check oil is sufficiently hot, add a 1.5cm cube of bread to pan – if it turns golden in 35 seconds, the oil is ready.) Working in batches, dust vegetables in flour and shake off excess. Dip in batter and allow excess to drip off, then add vegetables to oil, 6 at a time. Deep-fry for 1 minute, then, using a slotted metal spoon, turn vegetables over and cook for a further 2 minutes or until pale golden. Drain on paper towel, then place on oven tray and transfer to oven to keep warm. Dust prawns in flour and shake off excess. Dip in batter and allow excess to drip off. Deep-fry, in 2 batches, for 2 minutes or until pale golden and just cooked through. Drain on paper towel.

5 Divide tempura prawns and vegetables among bowls. Serve immediately with dipping sauce.

*See Cooking Notes, p 142

beef and vegetable rolls

Serves: 4
Preparation: 20 mins
Cooking: 15 mins

6 x 80g minute steaks
1 carrot, peeled
1 bunch asparagus
6 spring onions
12 toothpicks or
   small skewers
1 tbs cornflour
2 tbs vegetable oil
60ml (¼ cup) sake*
60ml (¼ cup) mirin*
60ml (¼ cup) Japanese
   soy sauce (shoyu)*
2 tsp caster sugar
Steamed short-grain rice*,
   to serve

1 Cut steaks in half widthwise. Place half the slices, side by side, between 2 sheets of plastic wrap and, using a meat mallet or rolling pin, pound until steaks are even and 3mm thick. Repeat with remaining beef.

2 Cut carrot lengthwise into 3 slices, then cut each slice into 4 batons. Trim to 10cm long. Trim asparagus and spring onion to the same length as the carrot batons, then cut each piece in half lengthwise.

3 To assemble beef rolls, place 1 slice of beef lengthwise on a clean work surface. Place 1 piece of carrot, spring onion and asparagus on top of beef. Roll up beef and secure with a toothpick. Repeat with remaining beef and vegetables. Sift half the cornflour over rolls, then turn rolls over and sift with remaining cornflour.

4 Heat 1 tbs oil in a large, non-stick frying pan, add 6 beef rolls and cook over medium heat for 3 minutes, turning occasionally, or until lightly browned. Transfer to a plate. Add remaining 1 tbs oil to pan and cook remaining 6 beef rolls. Transfer to a plate. Wipe frying pan clean with paper towel.

5 Heat frying pan over medium heat. Add sake, mirin, soy sauce, 60ml (¼ cup) water and sugar. Bring to the boil, and boil for 1 minute. Reduce heat to low–medium, return all beef rolls to the pan and simmer for 5 minutes, turning occasionally, or until cooked through. Transfer rolls to a plate. Increase heat to medium–high, bring sauce to the boil and cook for 1 minute or until slightly thickened. Return rolls to pan to glaze with sauce. Remove rolls from pan and set aside to rest for 2 minutes. Pour sauce over beef rolls and serve with steamed rice.

*See Cooking Notes, p 142

pork tonkatsu with sesame coleslaw

Serves: 4

Preparation: 25 mins
+ 30 mins refrigeration time

Cooking: 20 mins

100g (⅔ cup) plain flour
2 eggs
150g (2 cups) panko
  breadcrumbs*
4 x 150g pork leg steaks
Vegetable oil, to shallow-fry
  (see Mexican Cooking
  Notes, p 190)
Lemon wedges, to serve

Sesame coleslaw
½ small white onion
2 tbs sesame seeds
300g savoy cabbage
1 tsp vegetable oil
2 tbs rice vinegar*
1 tsp caster sugar
1 tsp Japanese soy
  sauce (shoyu)*

Tonkatsu sauce
2 tbs Worcestershire sauce
  (see English Cooking
  Notes, p 108)
60ml (¼ cup) tomato sauce
1 tbs Japanese soy sauce
2 tbs sake*
2 tsp rice vinegar*
¼ tsp mustard powder
  (see English Cooking
  Notes, p 108)

1 To make sesame coleslaw, cover onion with iced water and stand for 5 minutes. Drain on paper towel. Meanwhile, heat a frying pan over medium heat. Add sesame seeds and cook, stirring and shaking pan occasionally, for 5 minutes or until golden. Thinly shred cabbage and place in a bowl, add onion, cover with plastic wrap and refrigerate for at least 30 minutes. Just before serving, whisk together oil, vinegar, sugar and soy sauce in a bowl. Pour over cabbage mixture, add sesame seeds and toss to combine.

2 Meanwhile, to make tonkatsu sauce, place all ingredients in a saucepan and whisk to combine. Bring to the boil over high heat, then reduce to medium and simmer for 2 minutes. Cool.

3 Place flour in a bowl and season with salt and pepper. Crack eggs into another bowl and whisk gently. Place breadcrumbs in a third bowl. Dust pork steaks in seasoned flour, shaking off excess. Dip in egg, then coat in breadcrumbs, pressing down on both sides to help crumbs stick.

4 Heat 1cm oil in a deep frying pan over medium heat (get an adult to help you). Fry half the pork over medium heat for 4 minutes or until golden, then turn over and cook for a further 3 minutes or until golden and cooked through. Drain on paper towel. Cover loosely with foil and keep warm. Repeat with remaining pork.

5 Divide coleslaw among 4 plates. Cut each steak into 4 slices on the diagonal and place on coleslaw. Drizzle with tonkatsu sauce and serve with lemon wedges.

*See Cooking Notes, p 142

yakitori chicken and vegetables

Serves: 4
Preparation: 10 mins
Cooking: 15 mins

400g chicken thigh fillets
4 spring onions
24 bamboo skewers,
   soaked in water for
   30 minutes, drained
   (see Australian cooking
   notes, p 6)
12 button or shiitake
   mushrooms
1 bunch asparagus
Vegetable oil, to brush

Yakitori sauce
125ml (½ cup) Japanese
   soy sauce (shoyu)*
125ml (½ cup) mirin*
125ml (½ cup) sake*
2 tbs caster sugar

1 To make yakitori sauce, combine all ingredients in a saucepan and bring to the boil over high heat. Reduce heat to medium and simmer for 2 minutes or until sauce is slightly thickened. Cool.

2 Cut chicken into 2cm pieces and spring onions into 2cm lengths. Thread 3 pieces of chicken alternately with 2 pieces of spring onion onto 16 soaked bamboo skewers.

3 Trim stems and cut mushrooms in half. Cut asparagus into 3cm lengths. Thread 3 mushroom halves and 6 pieces of asparagus including 2 tips each onto 8 skewers.

4 Preheat a chargrill pan or barbecue to medium. Brush all skewers lightly with vegetable oil. Cook skewers, turning occasionally, for 3 minutes or until almost cooked through. Brush each skewer with yakitori sauce, return to grill or barbecue and cook for 1 minute each side, then repeat process twice more or until skewers are glazed and chicken and vegetables are cooked. Serve skewers with remaining yakitori sauce.

*See Cooking Notes, p 142

MIX & MATCH
Traditionally, yakitori refers to all foods that are skewered. Chicken is the most popular and is served in many ways from the grill, including wings.

TIME SAVER The yakitori sauce can be made a day ahead and stored, covered, in the refrigerator.

teriyaki salmon

Serves: 4

Preparation: 5 mins

+ 20 mins marinating time

Cooking: 10 mins

4 x 180g salmon fillets,
  skin on
2 tbs vegetable oil
Steamed short-grain rice*,
  to serve

Teriyaki sauce
125ml (½ cup) mirin*
60ml (¼ cup) sake*
80ml (⅓ cup) Japanese
  soy sauce (shoyu)*
2 tsp caster sugar

1 To make teriyaki sauce, combine mirin, sake, soy sauce and sugar in a small saucepan. Bring to the boil over medium heat and cook for 4 minutes or until slightly reduced. Cool.

2 To prepare salmon, using tweezers, carefully pull out any small bones remaining in the flesh (this is called 'pin-boning'). Place salmon, skin-side down, in a glass or ceramic dish. Pour cooled sauce over fish and marinate for 20 minutes.

3 Heat oil in a non-stick frying pan over high heat. Reduce heat to medium and cook drained salmon, skin-side down, for 3 minutes or until skin is crisp. Turn salmon over and cook for a further 2 minutes. Add 80ml (⅓ cup) teriyaki sauce, bring to a simmer, then spoon sauce over salmon to coat. Remove salmon from pan. Cut each into 3 pieces. Serve with green beans with sesame miso dressing (see recipe below) and steamed rice.

*See Cooking Notes, p 142

green beans with sesame miso dressing

Serves: 4

Preparation: 10 mins

Cooking: 10 mins

200g green beans, trimmed

Sesame miso dressing
35g (¼ cup) sesame seeds
1 tsp caster sugar
1½ tbs white miso paste*
2½ tbs mirin*

1 To make sesame miso dressing, heat a frying pan over medium heat. Add sesame seeds and cook, stirring and shaking pan occasionally, for 5 minutes or until golden. Reserve 2 tsp sesame seeds. Using a mortar and pestle, pound remaining sesame seeds until crushed. Add sugar, half the miso paste and mirin, and stir to combine, then gradually add remaining miso and mirin.

2 Cook beans in a saucepan of boiling salted water for 3 minutes or until tender. Drain under cold running water, then place in a bowl. Add dressing to beans and toss gently to combine. Serve scattered with reserved sesame seeds.

Morocco is at the tip of North Africa and looks across to Spain.

MOROC

Tangier

Casablanca ● Rabat

● Marrakech

MOROCCO

CO

THREE MOROCCAN
DIPS

*

BEEF KEBABS WITH
LEMON PILAF

*

LAMB AND DATE
TAGINE WITH HERBED
COUSCOUS

*

CHERMOULA FISH
WITH ORANGE SALAD

*

FIG AND WALNUT
CIGARS

MOROCCO COOKING NOTES

Have your mint tea with the fig and walnut cigars, page 168.

Moroccan mint tea

To make Moroccan mint tea, combine 1tbs loose green tea leaves or loose black tea leaves, 4 large sprigs mint and 1 tbs sugar in a teapot. Pour over 750ml (3 cups) boiling water, stir well and leave to brew for 5 minutes. Pour through a strainer into vsmall heatproof glasses. Serves 4.

ORANGE BLOSSOM WATER

Also known as orange flower water, this is a clear liquid made from distilling bitter orange blossoms. Available from Middle Eastern shops and delis.

FILO PASTRY

Unlike other pastry, filo is made from flour, water and a tiny amount of oil. Any fat is added later. As you work with each sheet of filo, cover remaining sheets with a slightly damp, clean tea towel to prevent them drying out. To slightly dampen a tea towel, flick it lightly with a little water, then wring it to dampen it evenly. Tightly wrap leftover filo in plastic wrap and refrigerate for another use.

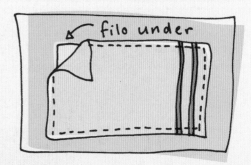

filo under

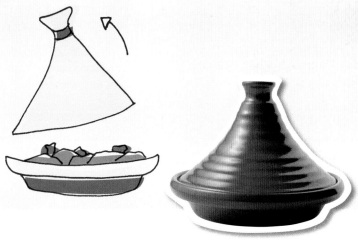

TAHINI

Tahini is a paste made from sesame seeds and is widely used in Middle Eastern cooking – from savoury dishes such as hummus to halva, a traditional sweet flavoured with honey and nuts, such as pistachios or almonds. It is available from supermarkets, delis and health food shops.

Tagines

These traditional clay cooking vessels also give the dish that's cooked inside them its name. They're ideal for slow-cooking, as the tall, conical lid causes all the moisture to drop back into the food that's cooking inside. The whole tagine is taken to the table, where the lid is removed before serving.

Ras el hanout

Ras el hanout, meaning 'top of the shop', is a Moroccan blend of up to 20 spices showing off a spice merchant's finest ingredients. It is available from selected delis and specialist food shops.

Make your own Combine 1 tsp ground cinnamon, 2 pinches ground white pepper, 1 tsp allspice, ½ tsp ground ginger, ½ tsp ground cardamom and ½ tsp ground turmeric in a screw-top jar and shake well to combine. Your ras el hanout will keep in a screw-top jar for up to 2 months.

three moroccan dips

Serves: 8
Preparation: 30 mins
+ 15 mins cooling time
Cooking: 20 mins

Flatbread and crudités
   (raw vegetable sticks),
   to serve

Spiced carrot dip
2 carrots, chopped
2 cloves garlic, peeled
½ tsp ground cumin
½ tsp ground turmeric
2 tsp lemon juice
2 tsp extra virgin olive oil

Muhumarra
2 red capsicums,
   quartered, seeded
½ tsp ground cumin
½ tsp sweet paprika
2 tsp lemon juice
2 tbs walnuts
2 tbs olive oil

Herbed tahini yoghurt
210g (¾ cup) Greek-style
   yoghurt
1 tbs tahini* (see Cooking
   Notes, p 158)
1 clove garlic, crushed
1 tbs chopped coriander
1 tbs chopped mint

1 To make spiced carrot dip, bring a saucepan of water to the boil over high heat. Add carrot and garlic, and simmer for 10 minutes or until softened. Drain well.

2 Place drained carrot mixture in a food processor. Add cumin, turmeric, lemon juice and oil, and process until smooth. Season with salt and pepper. Transfer to a bowl. Makes ¾ cup.

3 To make muhumarra, preheat grill to high. Line a large oven tray with foil and brush lightly with oil. Place capsicum quarters, skin-side up, on tray and grill for 10 minutes or until skin is blackened. Carefully wrap capsicums in the foil and set aside for 15 minutes or until cool enough to handle.

4 Peel charred skin from capsicums and discard. Place capsicums, cumin, paprika and lemon juice in a food processor. Process until smooth. Add walnuts and oil, and process until almost smooth. Season with salt and pepper. Transfer to a bowl. Makes 250ml (1 cup).

5 To make herbed tahini yoghurt, combine all ingredients in a bowl. Season with salt and pepper. Makes 250ml (1 cup).

6 Serve dips with flatbread and crudités. Dips will keep refrigerated in an airtight container for up to 3 days.

beef kebabs with lemon pilaf

Serves: 4

Preparation: 30 mins
+ 1 hr marinating time

Cooking: 25 mins

4 x 220g thick-cut sirloin
   steaks, trimmed of fat
2 tsp ras el hanout*
1 tbs olive oil
4 small red onions
8 button mushrooms,
   trimmed, if large, cut
   into quarters
1 red capsicum,
   quartered, seeded, cut
   into 4cm pieces
8 bamboo skewers, soaked
   in water for 30 minutes,
   drained (see Australian
   Cooking Notes, p 6)
Greek-style yoghurt, to serve

Lemon pilaf
1 tbs olive oil
1 tsp ras el hanout*
200g (1 cup) long-grain rice
375ml (1½ cups)
   chicken stock
1 tbs chopped
   preserved lemon rind
   (see Shopping List)
1 tbs chopped pitted
   green olives
1 tbs chopped flat-leaf
   parsley

1 Cut steak into 3cm cubes. You should get approximately 8 cubes per steak. Combine ras el hanout and oil in a bowl. Season with salt and pepper. Add steak and toss to combine. Cover with plastic wrap and marinate in the fridge for at least 1 hour or up to 8 hours.

2 To make lemon pilaf, heat oil in a saucepan over medium heat. Add ras el hanout and rice and cook, stirring, for 1 minute or until fragrant. Add stock and bring to the boil. Reduce heat to low and cover pan with a tight-fitting lid. Do not lift lid. Cook for 15 minutes or until liquid is absorbed. Remove pan from heat and stand, covered, for 10 minutes. Stir in preserved lemon, olives and parsley. Season with salt and pepper.

3 Meanwhile, preheat a barbecue or chargrill pan to high. Cut onions in half and then each half into 4 wedges to give 32. Thread meat, onion wedges, mushrooms and capsicum alternately onto 8 skewers. Brush meat and vegetables with a little oil. Season with salt and pepper. Cook skewers for 4 minutes each side or until meat is browned and tender. Serve beef kebabs with lemon pilaf and yoghurt.

*See Cooking Notes, p 158

SHOPPING LIST

Preserved lemons are available from delis. Only the rind is used. Using a small knife, cut away and discard the flesh, then chop the rind into small pieces. Substitute 1 tsp finely grated lemon zest if preserved lemon is unavailable.

lamb and date tagine with herbed couscous

Serves: 4
Preparation: 15 mins
Cooking: 1 hr 40 mins

1 tbs olive oil
2 onions, thinly sliced
3 cloves garlic, crushed
2 tsp ground cumin
1 tsp sweet paprika
1 tsp ground turmeric
½ tsp ground ginger
1kg diced lamb
400g can chopped
   tomatoes
250ml (1 cup) beef stock
2 cinnamon quills
1 tbs honey
6 fresh dates, halved, pitted
Coriander leaves, to serve

Herbed couscous
500ml (2 cups)
   chicken stock
1 tbs olive oil
250g (1¼ cups) couscous
25g butter
2 tbs chopped coriander

1 Heat oil in a large, heavy-based saucepan over low–medium heat. Add onions and cook, stirring occasionally, for 10 minutes or until softened and golden. Add garlic, spices and ginger and cook, stirring, for 2 minutes or until fragrant.

2 Add lamb and stir to coat in the onion mixture. Add tomatoes, stock and cinnamon quills. Bring to the boil, then reduce heat to low, cover, and simmer for 1 hour and 10 minutes or until lamb is almost tender.

3 Add the honey and dates and simmer, uncovered, for a further 20 minutes or until lamb is tender and sauce has thickened.

4 Meanwhile, to make herbed couscous, combine the stock and oil in a saucepan and bring to the boil over medium heat. Add the couscous, cover with a lid and remove pan from heat. Set aside for 5 minutes. Return the pan to low heat and add butter, fluffing couscous with a fork until butter is melted and grains are separated. Season with salt and pepper and stir in coriander.

5 Scatter lamb and date tagine with coriander leaves and serve with herbed couscous.

MIX & MATCH Chives or parsley would also make a lovely addition to the couscous.
CHEF'S TIP Like a curry, tagines can often taste better the next day as the flavours develop. Similarly, tagines can be made 2–3 days ahead.

chermoula fish with orange salad

Serves: 4
Preparation: 15 mins
Cooking: 10 mins

½ cup chopped coriander
½ cup chopped
   flat-leaf parsley
3 tsp finely grated
   lemon zest
2 cloves garlic, crushed
1 tsp sweet paprika
1 tsp ground cumin
60ml (¼ cup) olive oil
2 tbs lemon juice
4 x 150g firm white
   fish fillets such as
   blue-eye trevalla

Orange salad
2 oranges
2 tbs sliced pitted
   green olives
2 radishes, sliced
2 tbs olive oil

1 Preheat oven to 200C. Line an oven tray with baking paper. To make chermoula paste, combine coriander, parsley, lemon zest, garlic, paprika, cumin, olive oil and lemon juice in a small bowl. Season with salt and pepper.

2 Place fish on prepared tray. Coat both sides of fish with chermoula paste. Roast for 10 minutes (see Chef's Tips) or until just cooked through.

3 Meanwhile, to make orange salad (get an adult to help you), place an orange on a chopping board and slice off the top and base so it sits flat. Slice off the skin with the white pith, following the curve of the orange. Carefully slide the knife between the membrane walls towards the centre of orange to release the segments. Repeat with remaining orange. Combine orange segments, olives and radishes in a bowl. Drizzle with oil, season with salt and pepper and toss gently to combine. Serve orange salad with chermoula fish.

CHEF'S TIPS
• Add a little chilli powder or cayenne pepper to the chermoula if you like it spicy.
• Remember, the thicker the piece of fish, the longer it will take to cook.

fig and walnut cigars

Makes: 12
Preparation: 30 mins
Cooking: 30 mins

75g (¾ cup) walnuts
2 tbs caster sugar
½ tsp ground cinnamon
250g pre-soaked dried
   figs, quartered
9 sheets filo pastry*
125g unsalted butter,
   melted
2 tsp sesame seeds

Syrup
220g (1 cup) caster sugar
1 cinnamon quill
2 thin strips orange zest
2 tsp orange blossom
   water*

1 Place walnuts, sugar and cinnamon in a food processor. Using the pulse button, pulse until finely chopped. Add figs and pulse until chopped. Transfer mixture to a bowl.

2 Preheat oven to 200C. Line an oven tray with baking paper. Brush a sheet of filo pastry with butter, then top with a second sheet of filo. Brush with butter and top with a third sheet. Cut filo stack into 4 equal rectangles. Place 1 firmly packed tablespoon of fig mixture in a line 2cm up from a long edge and 2cm in from the sides of one filo stack. Fold pastry over filling and roll over once to enclose filling completely, then fold in both sides. Continue rolling to form a cigar shape. Repeat with remaining filo stacks, butter and filling to make 12 cigars. Sprinkle cigars with sesame seeds. Place on oven tray and bake for 20 minutes or until golden and crisp.

3 Meanwhile, to make syrup, combine sugar, cinnamon quill and orange zest with 250ml (1 cup) water in a small saucepan. Stir over medium heat until sugar dissolves. Bring to the boil, then reduce heat and simmer for 10 minutes or until reduced and syrupy. Stir in orange-blossom water. Drizzle syrup over fig and walnut cigars to serve.

*See Cooking Notes, p 158

CHEF'S TIP Store filo cigars and syrup separately in airtight containers at room temperature for up to 3 days.

THAILA

A popular snack in Thailand is deep-fried grasshoppers. They taste a bit like popcorn!

THAI FISH CAKES WITH
CUCUMBER RELISH

*

EGG NETS WITH PRAWNS

*

COCONUT CHICKEN SOUP

*

THAI BEEF SALAD

*

CHICKEN PAD THAI

*

DUCK RED CURRY
WITH PINEAPPLE

*

SALMON CHU CHEE WITH
PICKLED VEGETABLES

THAILAND COOKING NOTES

Thai basics

1 Lemongrass Its fragrant, grass-like leaves make a refreshing tea, but only the white part of the stem is used for cooking.

2 Galangal This root is related to the ginger family, for which it can be substituted. It needs to be peeled before using.

3 Kaffir lime leaves These highly scented leaves add a citrus tang to dishes. Substitute with the finely grated zest of 1 lime.

4 Red eschalots These onions are sweeter than regular ones. If you can't find them, French eschalots are a good substitute.

5 Coriander roots Coriander is sold as a bunch with the roots attached. Leaves, stems and roots are used in Thai cooking.

6 Thai basil This has a fresh, aniseed scent and flavour. Substitute with regular basil.

* All these ingredients are available from selected supermarkets, greengrocers and Asian grocers.

MORTAR AND PESTLE A mortar is a heavy bowl, usually made of stone such as granite. Also made of stone, the short, bat-like pestle is used to pound or grind ingredients in the bowl. Many cooks prefer this method to make pastes and grind spices, as it releases the fragrance and flavours more effectively than using a food processor.

MAKING EGG NETS

1 Using scissors, snip a 2–3mm hole in one of the bottom corners of a zip-lock bag.
2 Holding the bag as you would a piping bag, carefully drizzle egg through the hole into a frying pan from 10cm above the pan, quickly moving it from side to side one way, then across those lines at right angles, to form a thin, net-like effect.

CHEF'S TIP To shred kaffir lime leaves, stack them, roll up together tightly, then thinly slice with a knife.

Season to taste

Thai cooking follows a basic principle: the balance of four flavours – hot, salty, sour and sweet – should be in harmony.
1 Red curry paste This is the 'hot' spice base for many Thai dishes. You can also buy it ready-made.
2 Fish sauce The 'salty' flavouring for many Thai dishes, it is made by fermenting fish or shellfish products.
3 Belachan (shrimp paste) Ground shrimps fermented, then dried in the sun in blocks. Adds a 'sour-salty' flavour.
4 Palm sugar The 'sweet' element, made from boiling the sap of palm trees. Depending on the variety, its colour ranges from dark, almost black, to a creamy gold. It's sold in blocks, then grated for cooking. Substitute with brown sugar.
* All these ingredients are available from selected supermarkets and Asian grocers.

thai fish cakes with cucumber relish

Makes: 20

Preparation: 50 mins
+ 30 mins refrigeration time

Cooking: 8 mins

1 stalk lemongrass*, (white
part only), finely chopped

2 cloves garlic, chopped

2 kaffir lime leaves*,
shredded

2 coriander roots*,
finely chopped

2 long red chillies, seeded,
finely chopped

2 tbs coriander leaves

2 red eschalots*, peeled,
roughly chopped

½ small red capsicum,
seeded, roughly chopped

80ml (⅓ cup) fish sauce*

100ml coconut cream

2 tsp caster sugar

500g ling or snapper fillets,
roughly chopped

1 egg, lightly beaten

8 green beans, thinly sliced
into rounds

Vegetable oil, to shallow-fry
(see Mexican Cooking
Notes, p 190)

Cucumber relish, to serve
(see recipe, right)

1 Place lemongrass, garlic, lime leaves, coriander roots, chillies, coriander leaves, eschalots and capsicum in a food processor and process until finely chopped. Add fish sauce, coconut cream and sugar, and process for 20 seconds. Add fish and egg, and process for a further 30 seconds or until a smooth paste forms. Transfer to a bowl and stir in beans. Cover with plastic wrap and refrigerate for 30 minutes.

2 Line an oven tray with plastic wrap. Using your hands, form ¼ cupfuls of mixture into 20 x 5cm patties, wetting your hands between each patty to prevent the mixture from sticking, then place on prepared tray.

3 Heat 3cm oil in a large, deep frying pan over medium heat (get an adult to help you). Cook fish cakes, in 4 batches, for 1 minute each side or until golden and just cooked. Remove from pan with a slotted spoon and drain on paper towel. Serve Thai fishcakes immediately with cucumber relish.

*See Cooking Notes, p 172

CUCUMBER RELISH Stir 75g (⅓ cup) caster sugar, 125ml (½ cup) vinegar, a pinch of salt and 80ml (⅓ cup) water in a saucepan over medium heat until sugar dissolves. Simmer for 2 minutes. Remove from heat and cool. Place ½ a seeded, thinly sliced Lebanese cucumber, 3 thinly sliced red eschalots and 1 tbs coriander leaves in a bowl. Just before serving, pour over vinegar mixture and stir to combine.

egg nets with prawns

Serves: 4
Preparation: 25 mins
Cooking: 15 mins

4 eggs
2 tbs vegetable oil
3 coriander roots*, chopped
4 cloves garlic, chopped
2cm piece ginger, chopped
1kg medium green prawns,
    peeled, cleaned, chopped
    (see Australian Cooking
    Notes, p 6)
65g (¼ cup) light palm
    sugar*, finely chopped
    or grated
2 tbs fish sauce
1 stalk lemongrass* (white
    part only), thinly sliced
3 red eschalots*,
    thinly sliced
2 kaffir lime leaves*,
    shredded
1 long red chilli, seeded,
    thinly sliced
1 cup coriander leaves
½ cup mint leaves, roughly
    torn, if large
160g (2 cups) bean sprouts
Lime wedges, to serve

1 To make egg nets, whisk eggs in a bowl until combined, then strain into a zip-lock bag and seal. Using scissors, snip a 2–3mm hole in one of the bottom corners of the bag (see Cooking Notes, p 172). Heat 1 tbs oil in a large, non-stick frying pan and swirl to coat evenly. Holding the bag as you would a piping bag, drizzle one-quarter of egg through the hole into the pan from 10cm above the pan, quickly moving it from side to side one way, then across at right angles to form a thin, net-like effect. Cook over medium heat for 3 minutes or until egg net is set. Transfer to a plate. Repeat with remaining egg to make 4 nets.

2 Using a mortar and pestle (see Cooking Notes, p 172), pound coriander roots, garlic, ginger and a pinch of salt to a paste. Heat a wok over medium heat and add remaining 1 tbs oil. When hot, add garlic mixture and stir-fry for 30 seconds. Increase heat to high, add prawns and stir-fry for 2 minutes or until prawns change colour. Add palm sugar and fish sauce, and stir until sugar has dissolved and prawns are coated in the sauce. Cool for 10 minutes.

3 Combine lemongrass, eschalots, lime leaves, chilli, coriander, mint and bean sprouts in a bowl. Add prawn mixture and toss to combine. Place egg net on a plate, spoon one-quarter of prawn mixture on one half of egg net and fold other half over to cover. Repeat with remaining egg nets and prawn mixture. Serve with lime wedges.

*See Cooking Notes, p 172

coconut chicken soup

Serves: 4

Preparation: 30 mins

Cooking: 15 mins

2 stalks lemongrass*
   (white part only)
3 red eschalots*, peeled
2 coriander roots
   (see Chef's Tip)
2 red bird's-eye chillies
750ml (3 cups)
   chicken stock
250ml (1 cup) coconut milk
2 tsp caster sugar
50g galangal*, peeled,
   thinly sliced
6 kaffir lime leaves*
12 oyster mushrooms,
   roughly torn
115g pkt baby corn,
   halved lengthwise
400g chicken breast
   fillets, sliced
8 cherry tomatoes,
   halved
60ml (¼ cup) fish sauce*
1 lime, juiced
2 tbs coriander leaves

1 Using a mortar and pestle (see Cooking Notes, p 172), pound lemongrass, eschalots, coriander roots and chillies to bruise and release their fragrance. Set aside.

2 Combine stock and coconut milk in a saucepan over high heat and bring to the boil. Add sugar, galangal, lime leaves, and lemongrass mixture. Reduce heat to low and simmer, stirring occasionally, for 10 minutes.

3 Strain stock mixture, discarding solids. Return to pan, increase heat to high and bring to the boil. Add mushrooms, corn and chicken, then reduce heat to low and simmer for 5 minutes or until chicken is cooked through and vegetables are tender.

4 Add tomatoes, fish sauce and lime juice, and stir to combine. Serve coconut chicken soup scattered with coriander leaves.

*See Cooking Notes, p 172

CHEF'S TIP To prepare coriander roots, cut stems 1cm from the root, wash well and scrape white roots clean with a paring knife. Reserve leaves and stems for another use.

thai beef salad

Serves: 4
Preparation: 15 mins
+ 1 hr marinating time
Cooking: 6 mins

400g rump or sirloin steak
1 tbs fish sauce*
2 tbs oyster sauce
1 tsp caster sugar
½ small red onion,
    thinly sliced
8 cherry tomatoes, halved
½ cup coriander leaves
1 baby cos lettuce, leaves
    separated, roughly torn
    if large

Dressing
2 tbs fish sauce
2 tbs caster sugar
¼ cup lime juice, or to taste
1 stalk lemongrass*, (white
    part only), finely chopped
1 clove garlic, crushed
1 long red chilli, seeded,
    thinly sliced

1 Place steak in a dish. Combine fish sauce, oyster sauce and sugar in a small bowl and stir until sugar is dissolved. Rub mixture over both sides of beef, cover with plastic wrap and marinate in the fridge for 1 hour.

2 To make dressing, combine fish sauce, sugar, lime juice, lemongrass, garlic and chilli in a large bowl and whisk until sugar is dissolved.

3 Heat a lightly oiled chargrill pan or barbecue to medium-high. Cook beef for 3 minutes each side for medium-rare. Transfer to a plate, cover loosely with foil and rest for 10 minutes. Slice beef and add it to dressing with any cooking juices. Add onion, tomatoes and coriander, and toss to combine.

4 To serve, place lettuce leaves on a plate and top with beef mixture.

*See Cooking Notes, p 172

CHEF'S TIP For a spicier dish, leave the seeds in the long red chilli.

chicken pad thai

Serves: 4

Preparation: 35 mins
+ 30 mins marinating time

Cooking: 10 mins

400g chicken breast
   fillets, sliced
2 tsp caster sugar
80ml (⅓ cup) fish sauce
250g dried rice
   stick noodles
90g (⅓ cup) light palm
   sugar*, grated
85g (¼ cup) tamarind purée
   (see Indian Cooking
   Notes, p 92)
60ml (¼ cup) vegetable oil
6 (50g) red eschalots*,
   peeled, roughly chopped
2 eggs, lightly beaten
35g (¼ cup) roasted
   unsalted peanuts,
   chopped
65g (1 cup) bean sprouts
¾ bunch garlic chives,
   cut into 2cm lengths
Extra bean sprouts,
   chopped roasted peanuts,
   garlic chives, and lime
   wedges and chilli flakes,
   to serve

1 Place chicken, caster sugar and 1 tbs fish sauce in a bowl and stir to combine. Cover with plastic wrap and marinate in the fridge for 30 minutes.

2 Place noodles in a bowl, cover with water and soak for 10 minutes to soften. Drain. Bring a large saucepan of water to the boil and cook noodles for 2 minutes, stirring occasionally. Drain and set aside.

3 Place palm sugar, tamarind purée and remaining 60ml (¼ cup) fish sauce in a bowl, add 2 tbs water and whisk until sugar is dissolved.

4 Heat a wok over high heat and add 1 tbs oil. When very hot, add chicken and stir-fry for 2 minutes or until chicken is browned. Transfer to a plate. Wipe wok clean. Heat wok over medium heat and, when hot, add remaining 2 tbs oil. Add eschalots and stir-fry for 30 seconds. Add eggs and cook, without stirring, for 30 seconds or until egg has just set. Increase heat to high, add noodles and toss to combine, breaking up the egg with a spoon (be careful not to break the noodles). Stir-fry for 1 minute, then add chicken, ¼ cup peanuts and tamarind mixture, and stir-fry for a further 2 minutes or until liquid has been absorbed by the noodles. Add bean sprouts and chives, and toss for 30 seconds or until well combined. Serve chicken pad Thai with extra bean sprouts, peanuts, chives, and lime wedges and chilli flakes.

*See Cooking Notes, p 172

duck red curry
with pineapple

Serves: 4
Preparation: 45 mins
Cooking: 20 mins

125ml (½ cup)
  coconut cream
2 tbs vegetable oil
100g red curry paste
  (see recipe, below)
1 cinnamon quill
4 kaffir lime leaves*
2 tbs fish sauce*
1½ tbs light palm
  sugar*, grated
180ml (¾ cup) coconut milk
1 long red chilli, seeded,
  thickly sliced
½ store-bought Chinese
  barbecue duck, chopped
100g peas or snow
  peas, trimmed
½ small pineapple,
  peeled, cored, cut into
  bite-size pieces
3 tsp lime juice
½ cup Thai basil leaves*
Steamed rice, to serve

1 Place coconut cream and oil in a large, heavy-based frying pan and bring to the boil over medium–high heat. Cook, stirring continuously, for 5 minutes or until oil separates from cream.

2 Reduce heat to low–medium, add red curry paste, cinnamon and kaffir lime leaves, and cook, stirring frequently, for 10 minutes to cook out the raw taste of the spices.

3 Add fish sauce and palm sugar, and stir until sugar dissolves. Add coconut milk, chilli and 250ml (1 cup) water. Increase heat to medium and bring to the boil, stirring continuously. Add duck and simmer for 3 minutes. Add peas and pineapple, and simmer for a further 30 seconds or until warmed through. Remove from heat, stir in lime juice and half the basil leaves. Scatter duck red curry with remaining basil leaves and serve with steamed rice.

*See Cooking Notes, p 172

RED CURRY PASTE Soak 1 dried long red chilli in boiling water for 8 minutes, then drain, seed and roughly chop. Place in a food processor with 2 stalks roughly chopped lemongrass* (white part only), 2cm piece peeled, chopped galangal*, 1 seeded, roughly chopped fresh long red chilli, 3 chopped cloves garlic, 8 chopped red eschalots, zest of 1 lime, 1 tsp belachan*, ¼ tsp each of ground coriander and cumin, ½ tsp sweet paprika and 1 tbs vegetable oil and process to a smooth paste. Place paste in a screw-top jar, pour over a thin layer of vegetable oil to cover, then seal and refrigerate for up to 1 week.

salmon chu chee with pickled vegetables

Serves: 4

Preparation: 50 minutes
+ 30 mins marinating time

Cooking: 30 mins

125ml (½ cup)
   coconut cream
2 tbs vegetable oil
1 quantity Thai red curry
   paste (see recipe, p 184)
4 kaffir lime leaves*,
   shredded
2 tbs fish sauce
1½ tbs palm sugar*
160ml (⅔ cup) coconut milk
3 tsp lime juice
½ cup loosely packed
   Thai basil leaves*
4 x 200g skinless salmon
   fillets, pin-boned
   (see recipe, p 154)
1 long red chilli, seeded,
   finely sliced

Pickled vegetables
125ml (½ cup) white vinegar
110g (½ cup) caster sugar
½ pkt (60g) baby corn,
   halved lengthwise
1 small carrot, thinly sliced
100g wombok, sliced
   (see Chinese Cooking
   Notes, p 74)
½ Lebanese cucumber, sliced
   lengthwise into ribbons
8 cherry tomatoes, halved

1 To make the pickled vegetables, combine vinegar, sugar and 125ml (½ cup) water in a small saucepan over medium heat and stir until sugar dissolves. Increase heat to high and bring to the boil, then remove from heat and set aside to cool. Place corn, carrot and wombok in a bamboo steamer, cover and cook over a pan of simmering water for 1 minute or until vegetables are just tender. Combine steamed vegetables, vinegar mixture, cucumber and cherry tomatoes in a bowl. Cover with plastic wrap and marinate in the fridge for 30 minutes. Strain.

2 Place coconut cream and oil in a large heavy-based frying pan and bring to the boil over medium–high heat. Cook, stirring continuously, for 5 minutes or until oil separates from cream.

3 Reduce heat to low–medium, add curry paste and half the lime leaves, and cook, stirring frequently, for 10 minutes or until fragrant. Add fish sauce and palm sugar, and stir until sugar dissolves. Add coconut milk, increase heat to high and bring to the boil, stirring continuously. Remove from heat and stir in lime juice and half the basil leaves.

4 Heat a lightly oiled chargrill pan or a large frying pan over medium heat and cook salmon for 4 minutes each side or until just cooked. Divide salmon and sauce among plates and scatter with chilli and remaining basil and kaffir lime leaves. Serve with pickled vegetables.

*See Cooking Notes, p 172

TIME SAVER Substitute curry paste with 80g purchased red curry paste, but add half the amount of palm sugar and fish sauce, adjusting as necessary, depending on the paste that is used.

Tijuana

MEXICO

Cancún

Mexico City

Acapulco

MEXICO

TOSTADAS WITH
TOMATO SALSA AND
GUACAMOLE

*

CORN AND CHEESE
EMPANADAS

*

CHICKEN ENCHILADAS

*

FISH BURRITOS
WITH CABBAGE SALAD
AND AVOCADO CREAM

*

CHILLI CON CARNE

*Mexicans eat
300 million corn
tortillas daily!*

MEXICO COOKING NOTES

Cutting corn kernels from the cob

Using an oven glove or folded clean tea towel, hold the cob upright on a chopping board with one hand. Holding a knife in the other hand, cut down the length of the cob between the base of the kernels and the 'honeycombed' core. Keep cutting downwards, rotating the cob, until all the kernels have been removed.

FRYING

Make sure there's an adult with you when you're frying, as cooking with hot oil can be dangerous. The pan should be dry before you add the oil or it will spit. Don't crowd the pan with food, as the oil may bubble over, and always use long tongs to lower the food into the oil and turn it.

TORTILLAS These are a staple in Mexico and are made with either corn (maize) or wheat flour. You can buy them in supermarkets. Use the flour ones for making burritos (p 198), as they're bigger and don't tend to split as easily.

CHILLIES – FRESH OR DRY?

Chillies come in many shapes and sizes, from mild to super-hot and, while you can interchange fresh or dried ones in most recipes, they *do* have different flavours. However, drying them doesn't change how hot your chilli will be. The hottest part of the chilli is the membrane that holds the seeds in place, so if you want a milder flavour, be sure to remove this as well as the seeds.

CHOP CHOP Wear disposable gloves to chop chillies. If you do accidentally touch chillies with bare hands, wash your hands immediately and don't touch your eyes. Add a small amount of chilli to your dish, then taste it before you add any more, so you can get the right level of spice for your taste.

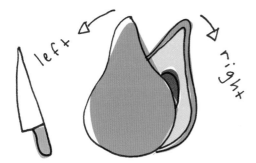

Removing an avocado stone

Using a sharp knife, carefully cut all the way around the avocado lengthwise through to the stone. Twist each half of the avocado in opposite directions to separate them, then scoop out the stone with a spoon and discard.

tostadas with tomato salsa and guacamole

Serves: 4
Preparation: 20 mins
Cooking: 5 mins

400g can refried beans
   (see Shopping List)
½ tsp ground cumin
Vegetable oil, to
   shallow-fry*
8 x 15cm white
   corn tortillas*
4 cos lettuce leaves,
   thinly sliced
160g (¾ cup) feta, crumbled

Tomato salsa

2 vine-ripened tomatoes
2 tbs chopped coriander
½ long red chilli, seeded,
   finely chopped* (optional)
1 clove garlic,
   finely chopped
1 tbs lime juice
1 tbs olive oil

Guacamole

1 large avocado, stone
   removed*
1 tbs lime juice
½ small red onion,
   finely chopped
¼ tsp ground cumin

1 To make tomato salsa, cut tomatoes in half widthwise and using a spoon, scoop out and discard seeds. Chop flesh and place in a bowl. Add remaining ingredients, season with salt and pepper, then toss to combine.

2 To make guacamole, place avocado and lime juice in a bowl and mash with a fork. Add onion and cumin, season with salt and pepper and stir to combine.

3 To cook bean purée, combine beans, cumin and 2 tbs water in a saucepan and stir over low–medium heat until smooth. Season with salt and pepper.

4 Preheat oven to 100C. Heat 1cm oil in a frying pan over medium heat (get an adult to help you). Using tongs, place tortillas, one at a time, in hot oil for 15 seconds or until puffed and golden. Turn over and cook for a further 10 seconds. Drain on paper towel. Place on an oven tray lined with baking paper and keep warm in oven. Repeat with remaining tortillas.

5 Spread bean purée on warm tortillas, top with lettuce, guacamole and a spoonful of salsa. Scatter with crumbled feta and serve immediately.

*See Cooking Notes, p 190

MIX & MATCH Top tostadas with shredded cooked chicken breast or chopped cooked prawn meat.
SHOPPING LIST Refried beans are available from the Mexican aisle in selected supermarkets.

corn and cheese empanadas

Makes: 12

Preparation: 15 mins
+ 45 mins resting time

Cooking: 55 mins

2 small desiree potatoes
2 cobs corn
2 tbs vegetable oil
1 onion, sliced
1 clove garlic
60g (½ cup) grated
　cheddar
65g (⅓ cup) crumbled feta
1 egg, lightly beaten with
　1 tbs water, for egg wash

Pastry

80g butter, chopped
350g (2⅓ cups) plain flour
1 egg

CHEF'S TIP Empanadas are a snack or street food and are often deep-fried. To deep-fry empanadas (get an adult to help you and see Cooking Notes, p 190), follow recipe to Step 5, but do not brush pastry with egg wash. Heat vegetable oil to 160C (when a cube of bread turns golden in 2½ minutes) and deep-fry empanadas, in batches, for 5 minutes or until golden and puffed.

1 To make pastry, combine 200ml water, butter and 1 tsp salt in a saucepan and stir over medium heat until butter has melted. Sift flour into a bowl, make a well in the centre, then pour in butter mixture. Add egg and mix with a dinner knife to a soft dough.

2 Transfer dough to a lightly floured work surface. Knead until smooth and elastic, and no longer sticky. Place in a clean bowl, cover with a clean tea towel and set aside for 45 minutes.

3 Steam unpeeled potatoes in a covered steamer over a saucepan of boiling water for 10 minutes. Add corn and steam for a further 5 minutes or until potatoes and corn are just tender. Cool for 10 minutes. Peel potatoes and cut into 1cm cubes. Cut kernels from corn (see Cooking Notes, p 190).

4 Heat oil in a frying pan over low heat, add onion and cook for 5 minutes or until softened. Add garlic, steamed potatoes and corn. Increase heat to medium and cook, stirring occasionally, for 8 minutes or until lightly browned. Transfer mixture to a bowl, add cheeses, and stir to combine.

5 Preheat oven to 180C. Line an oven tray with baking paper. Divide dough into 12 pieces. Roll each piece on a lightly floured surface into a 10cm round. Place a heaped tablespoon of mixture onto each round. Brush the edge of the pastry with water, fold each round in half and, using a fork, crimp edges to seal. Brush empanadas with egg wash and place on the oven tray. Bake for 25 minutes or until golden. Serve immediately.

chicken enchiladas

Serves: 4

Preparation: 30 mins
+ 20 mins cooling time

Cooking: 1 hr 10 mins

500g chicken breast fillets
1 onion, halved
2 cloves garlic, peeled
2 sprigs flat-leaf parsley
1 red capsicum, quartered,
    seeded
200g (1 cup) crumbled feta
¼ tsp ground cumin
8 x 15cm corn tortillas (see
    Cooking Notes, p 190)
8 toothpicks
60g (½ cup) grated cheddar
Coriander leaves, to serve

Roasted tomato sauce

1 long red chilli
1kg vine-ripened tomatoes
1 tbs olive oil
1 small onion, finely
    chopped
2 cloves garlic, finely
    chopped

CHEF'S TIP For those who
like extra heat, leave the
seeds in the chilli.

1 Place chicken, onion, garlic and parsley in a saucepan. Add enough cold water to cover chicken. Bring to the boil over medium heat. Reduce heat to low and simmer for 10 minutes. Remove pan from heat and stand for 5 minutes. Remove chicken from stock. Strain stock and reserve. Cool chicken for 10 minutes, then roughly chop and place in a bowl.

2 To make sauce, heat a barbecue or chargrill pan over high heat. Pierce chilli with a knife to prevent it bursting. Chargrill whole tomatoes and chilli, turning frequently, or until skins are charred. Transfer to a chopping board and cool for 5 minutes. When cool, peel skins from tomatoes and chilli. Discard stem from chilli, cut in half lengthwise and remove seeds. Process chilli and tomatoes in a food processor to a purée.

3 Heat oil in a large frying pan over low-medium heat, add onion and cook for 5 minutes. Add garlic and cook for 3 minutes. Add tomato mixture and 180ml (¾ cup) reserved chicken stock and bring to the boil. Reduce heat and simmer for 20 minutes or until thickened. Transfer to a shallow dish.

4 Meanwhile, preheat grill to high. Place capsicum, skin-side up, on a foil-lined tray and grill for 8 minutes or until skin blackens. Wrap in foil and stand for 10 minutes. Peel and roughly chop. Add to chicken with 125g feta and cumin. Season and toss to combine.

5 Preheat oven to 180C. Dip a tortilla in sauce, turn over and dip other side. Place on a clean work surface and place ⅓ cup chicken mixture along centre of tortilla. Roll up tortilla and secure with a toothpick. Place, seam-side up, in a shallow, 3-litre (12-cup) ovenproof dish. Repeat with remaining tortillas, sauce and chicken mixture. Spoon remaining sauce over tortillas and sprinkle with remaining feta and grated cheddar. Bake for 30 minutes or until cheese is golden bubbling. Scatter with coriander to serve.

fish burritos with cabbage salad and avocado cream

Serves: 4

Preparation: 15 mins

Cooking: 10 mins

1 tsp ground cumin

½ tsp dried oregano

500g flathead fillets,
   pin-boned (see Chef's Tip)

4 large flour tortillas*

60ml (¼ cup) vegetable oil

1 lime, quartered, plus extra
   lime wedges, to serve

Cabbage salad

160g red cabbage, finely
   shredded

2 tomatoes, chopped

¼ cup coriander leaves

3 tsp lime juice

Avocado cream

1 large avocado,
   stone removed*

1 tbs sour cream

2 tsp lime juice

1 To make cabbage salad, combine all ingredients in a bowl. Season with salt and pepper. Set aside.

2 To make avocado cream, mash avocado with a fork, add sour cream and lime juice, then mash until smooth. Season with salt and pepper. Cover with plastic wrap and refrigerate.

3 Combine cumin and oregano in a bowl. Season with salt and pepper. Place fish fillets on a chopping board and sprinkle both sides with mixture.

4 Preheat oven to 150C. Heat a heavy-based frying pan over medium heat. Add 1 tortilla and cook for 25 seconds each side or until warmed through, then transfer to a plate. Cover loosely with foil and transfer to oven to keep warm. Repeat with remaining tortillas.

5 Meanwhile, heat oil in a heavy-based frying pan over medium heat. Cook fish, in 2 batches, for 2 minutes each side (depending on thickness) or until just cooked (the flesh will be opaque and flake easily with a fork). Transfer to a plate lined with paper towel and cool slightly. Break into bite-size pieces.

6 Place warm tortillas on a work surface, spoon cabbage salad along centre of tortilla, top with fish pieces and spoon over avocado cream. Squeeze a lime quarter over each burrito, fold over and serve immediately with extra lime wedges.

*See Cooking Notes, p 190

CHEF'S TIP To pin-bone fish, use tweezers to pull out any small bones that may be left in the flesh.

chilli con carne

Serves: 4
Preparation: 30 mins
Cooking: 2 hrs 40 mins

2 long red chillies* (see
   Cooking Notes, p 190)
80ml (⅓ cup) vegetable oil
1.5kg beef chuck steak, cut
   into 3cm pieces
2 onions, chopped
2 cloves garlic, chopped
2 tsp ground cumin
1 tsp dried oregano
2 x 400g cans
   chopped tomatoes
250ml (1 cup) beef stock
½ cup chopped coriander
Steamed rice and sour
   cream, to serve

1 Using a knife, cut chillies in half lengthwise, then, using a small spoon, scoop out seeds and discard. Finely chop chillies.

2 Heat a large saucepan over medium–high heat. Add 1 tbs oil and cook beef, in 3 batches, for 5 minutes or until browned all over, adding 1 tbs oil with each batch. Transfer beef to a plate, reserving saucepan.

3 Reduce heat to low, add remaining 1 tbs oil to same saucepan and cook onions, stirring occasionally, for 5 minutes or until lightly browned. Increase heat to medium, add chillies, garlic, cumin, oregano and 60ml (¼ cup) water and cook, stirring, with a wooden spoon, scraping any pieces from the base of the pan. Simmer for 2 minutes. Add tomatoes, beef and stock, and stir to combine. Season with salt and pepper. Reduce heat to low, then cover with a lid and cook, stirring occasionally, for 1½ hours. Remove lid, increase heat to low-medium and cook for a further 45 minutes or until meat is very tender and sauce is thickened. Stir in coriander. Serve chilli con carne with steamed rice and sour cream.

CHEF'S TIP
For a mild chilli con carne, halve the quantity of chillies, or, for a spicier dish, leave the seeds in the chillies.
MIX & MATCH Serve chilli con carne with the tomato salsa from the tostadas recipe on page 192.

COOKING BASICS

Baking

Oven temperatures are for conventional ovens. Reduce by 20 degrees for fan-forced ovens. When baking, have all your equipment ready and your ingredients at room temperature before you start.

Chocolate

- Cocoa solids give chocolate its flavour. Dark chocolate has a higher percentage of cocoa solids than milk chocolate. Choose a product that contains 55% to 85%, depending on how bitter you like your chocolate. Avoid chocolate with any added butter or oil, as it's not suitable for cooking.
- To melt chocolate, fill a saucepan one-third full with water and bring to a gentle simmer. Place the chopped chocolate in a heatproof bowl, place over pan and stir until chocolate melts. (Don't let the bowl touch the water.)

Cream

Pouring cream (35% butter fat) is suitable for sauces.
Thickened cream (35% butter fat) contains gelatine and is most suitable for whipping.
Double cream (48% butter fat or more) is usually for serving.

Eggs

- We recommend using eggs laid by free-range poultry.
- Use eggs at room temperature.
- Unless specified, all eggs used are 59g (extra large).

Ghee

Ghee is a form of clarified butter that's been simmered until the milk solids begin to brown, giving it a nutty, caramel flavour before they're removed. A staple of Indian cooking, it can be heated to higher temperatures than regular butter without burning and is available from supermarkets.

Hygiene

- Always wash your hands before you start cooking and don't dry wet or sticky hands on your clothes – use a clean tea towel or paper towel.
- Always scrub your nails before and after cooking.
- Wear an apron (or clothes you don't mind getting dirty) so you don't stain what you are wearing.

Knives

A blunt knife is a dangerous knife – you have to apply much more pressure to cut through food, so if the knife slips, you could cut yourself badly. With a sharp knife, very little pressure is needed to glide through the food, so any mishaps are likely to result in a small cut. The safest cutting techniques are the bridge and claw methods (see opposite page).

Measuring capacity

To measure the capacity of a dish, place dish in the sink. Fill a measuring jug with water and measure the capacity of the dish by the amount of water it takes to fill it to the very top.

Cooking oils

Refined oils, such as vegetable oil, are best for frying as they have a high smoke point

Bridge

Claw

CUTTING TECHNIQUES

- BRIDGE Form a 'bridge' with the thumb and the index finger of one hand and hold the item on a chopping board with the flattest part down. Hold a paring knife in the other hand and position the blade under the bridge, then cut down firmly.
- CLAW Place the item you want to cut flat-side down on a chopping board. Tuck the thumb inside the fingers of one hand and shape into a 'claw', then rest on the item. Hold the knife in the other hand and slice, moving the clawed fingers away as cutting progresses.

(the temperature they reach before they start to break up and 'smoke'). Olive oil has a far lower smoke point and is more suitable for salad dressings and sautéing.

Onions

We refer to these varieties:
Onions are the regular brown variety.
Red onions (sometimes known as Spanish onions).
Spring onions are the long, thin, green variety.

Bulb spring onions are the long, thin, green variety with the white bulb.
Eschalots are the small, sweet variety with the golden-coloured skin.

Refreshing

Refreshing vegetables or fruit preserves their colour and texture, while removing the raw flavour. After blanching or par-cooking, drop them immediately into iced water to halt the cooking process.

Seasoning

Unless stated otherwise, 'season' means to season with salt and pepper. For the best flavour, use sea salt and freshly ground black pepper from a grinder. Always season lightly so you don't overwhelm the flavour.

Supervision

It is a good idea to have adult supervision when cooking, especially if you're using knives or handling hot items.

INDEX

HarperCollins*Publishers*
First published in Australia in 2012 by
HarperCollins*Publishers* Australia Pty Ltd
ABN 36 009 913 517
harpercollins.com.au

HarperCollins*Publishers*
13/201 Elizabeth Street, Sydney, NSW 2000, Australia
31 View Road, Glenfield, Auckland 0627, New Zealand

National Library of Australia cataloguing-in-publication entry. Junior MasterChef (Television program).
Junior MasterChef Cookbook. Volume 2/Junior MasterChef. 9780732294274 (Pbk). Includes index. For primary
school age. Subjects: Junior MasterChef (Television program). Cooking, Australia-Juvenile literature. 641.5994

Produced by News Magazines
Editor-in-chief Trudi Jenkins **Food Director** Sophia Young **Managing Editor** Sally Feldman
Creative Director Scott Cassidy **Project Art Director** Jacqui Porter **Project Sub-editor** Robin Hill
Photography Jeremy Simons **Styling** Berni Smithies **Project Food Director** Bronwen Warden
Recipes writers Cynthia Black, Claudia Dunlop, Syd Pemberton, Jan Purser, Dimitra Stais, Bronwen Warden
Project Food Editor Julie Ballard **Project Food Editor's Assistants** Rebecca Truda, Arum Shim
Illustrations Stephanie Westcott
Group Publisher, Food Fiona Nilsson **Chief Executive Officer** Sandra Hook

Cover design HarperCollins*Publishers*

All meat supplied by Craig Cook's Prime Quality Meats (primequalitymeat.com.au)
Props supplied by Japan City (02 9387 8586), Mao & More (maoandmore.com),
Market Import (marketimport.com.au), Thonet (thonet.com.au)

Colour reproduction by Graphic Print Group, Adelaide
Printed and bound in China by RR Donnelley on 128gsm matt art

1 2 3 4   12 13 14

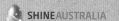

Australia
Spain
Italy
Greece
China
India
England
France
Japan
Morocco
Thailand
Mexico